A WALKER'S GUIDE

ZOE TEHRANI'S BRITAIN:
A WALKER'S GUIDE

30 Walks
From London Using Public Transport

Synergy Publishing
Newberry, FL 32669
publishwithsynergy.com

Zoe Tehrani's Britain, A Walker's Guide
By Zoe Tehrani

Copyright© 2025 by Zoe Tehrani

All rights reserved. Under International Copyright Law, no part of this publication may be reproduced, stored, or transmitted by any means–electronic, mechanical, photographic (photocopy), recording, or otherwise–without written permission from the publisher and copyright holder.
Printed in the United Kingdom.
International Standard Book Number: ISBN 9781610369176

Interior Layout Design: Cris Convery
hello@crisconvery.com

The information contained in this book is for general informational and educational purposes only. While every effort has been made to ensure the accuracy and reliability of the content, the author and publisher make no guarantees regarding the results that may be obtained from following the advice or practices described herein.

Walking is generally a safe activity, but it may not be suitable for everyone. Readers are encouraged to consult with a physician or other qualified health care provider before beginning any new exercise program, especially if they have any underlying health conditions, injuries, or concerns.

The author and publisher disclaim any liability for any loss, injury, or damage resulting directly or indirectly from the use or misuse of the information provided in this book.

Always use common sense, be aware of your surroundings, and prioritize your personal safety when walking in any environment.

CONTENTS

South Downs National Park

1 BLACK DOWN TEMPLE OF THE WINDS *p16*
9 miles/14 km – The highest hill in the South Downs National Park, heather, views

2 HASSOCKS TO LEWES VIA DITCHLING BEACON *p30*
10 miles/16 km – The South Downs Way ridge, an Iron Age hill fort, the highest point in East Sussex, a charming medieval town

3 AMBERLEY TO BIGNOR HILL *p42*
8.5 miles/13.5 km – Fairytale woods, a river, views

4 HASSOCKS TO DEVIL'S DYKE *p50*
9.5 miles/15.5 km – The longest, deepest, widest dry valley in the UK

5 LEWES CIRCULAR VIA SOUTHEASE *p62*
11.5 miles/18.5 km – The South Downs Way, views, ancient ruins, river

6 SOUTHEASE TO SEAFORD VIA ALFRISTON *p74*
14.5 miles/23.5 km – The South Downs Way, a historic village, chalk white cliffs, the sea

7 AMBERLEY TO ARUNDEL ALONG THE RIVER ARUN *p86*
6 mies/9.5 km – River, a castle, a historic market town

Surrey Hills National Landscape

8 HASLEMERE TO DEVIL'S PUNCH BOWL *p98*
7 miles/11 km – A massive natural amphitheatre full of wildlife, big hills

9 GUILDFORD, ST MARTHA'S HILL, AND NEWLANDS CORNER *p114*
11.5 miles/18.5 km – A hilltop church, ancient woods, gunpowder mills, stargazing hill

10 LEITH HILL: HOLMWOOD TO DORKING *p128*
12 miles/19 km – Highest point in South East England, views to London, a vineyard, woods

11 BOX HILL AND THE STEPPING STONES *p138*
3.5 miles/5.5km – A big hill, lots of steps, amazing views

12 GUILDFORD TO GODALMING ALONG THE RIVER WEY *p150*
6 miles/9.5 km – A river with history

Chilterns National Landscape

13 WENDOVER, COOMBE HILL, AND CHEQUERS *p162*
7 miles/11 km – The second highest hill in the Chilterns, lots of views, the Prime Minister's country home

14 HENLEY-ON-THAMES TO ASTON AND STONOR PARK *p174*
8 miles/13 km – Posh market town, white deer, River Thames

15 TRING TO INVINGHOE BEACON VIA ALDBURY *p186*
9 miles/14.5 km – An Iron Age Hill fort, chalk lion, amazing views

16 HENLEY-ON-THAMES TO GREYS COURT *p198*
8 miles/13 km – Posh town, a Tudor country house, vast woods

High Weald National Landscape

17 OUSE VALLEY VIADUCT AND THE ARDINGLY RESERVOIR p212
8 miles/13 km – A photogenic viaduct, pretty reservoir, fields

18 ETCHINGHAM TO ROBERTSBRIDGE VIA BODIAM CASTLE p224
11.5 miles/18.5 km – A moated castle, oast houses, farms

19 HASTINGS TO RYE p236
12.5 miles/20 km – Coast, hills, a medieval village

20 TUNBRIDGE WELLS TO ERIDGE ROCKS p250
14 miles/22.5 km – Big rocks outcrops, steam trains, woodland

21 THE FOREST WAY: EAST GRINSTEAD TO GROOMBRIDGE p264
11 miles/17.5 km – Lots of trees, old railway line, Winnie the Pooh

Kent Downs National Landscape

22 WYE TO DEVIL'S KNEADING TROUGH p276
5 miles/8 km – An idyllic village, nature reserve, white chalk hill figure, a steep dry valley

23 SHOREHAM CIRCULAR VIA OTFORD p286
8 miles/13 km – A white chalk hill figure, views to London, a Heritage Village and Grade II listed duck pond

24 KNOLE PARK AND INGTHAM MOTE p298
11 miles/17.5 km – Deer, a manor house, a moated house

South East Coast Path

25 MARGATE TO RAMSGATE VIA BROADSTAIRS p312
9 miles/14.5 km – The best sandy beaches on the South East Coast, medieval towns

26 DOVER TO DEAL p326
11 miles/17.5 km – White cliffs of Dover, clifftop meadows, beach

27 SEVEN SISTERS CLIFFS: SEAFORD TO EASTBOURNE p336
13.5 miles/21.5 km – White chalk cliffs, lots of hills, one of the best views along the South East Coast

28 FOLKESTONE TO DOVER p348
9 miles/14.5 km – A cliffside winding trail, war history

29 NEWHAVEN TO BRIGHTON p358
11.5 miles/18.5 km – Cliffs, under cliff path and Mr Bean steps

30 HERNE BAY TO MARGATE p368
12.5 miles/20 km – Medieval ruins, long promenade, beaches, curvy cliffs

Hello.

Hello, my name is Zoe. Welcome to my guide of the best walks from London. I am a physiotherapist who started hiking in 2016 to help with depression. Actually, let's go back a little...

My Story

In 2014 I took a career break and went backpacking for six months around South East Asia and the South Pacific. When I returned home to London I got very depressed. The kind where I didn't get out of bed unless I had to. It took about a year before I saw my GP, and went on to antidepressants.

After a few months and starting to feel a bit better, I took a trip back to SE Asia to the Perhentian Islands, with a stopover in Hong Kong. Whilst there I caught a train out of the city to do a hike. It was the most incredible journey, with views back to the city skyline, and it was just so easy. The logistics, that is, not the hike – that was tough.

One minute I was in the chaotic city, next I was out surrounded by nature, and then back on a train into the city. I started to wonder if London was the same. Could I get a train out of London to hike for the day? Was there even anywhere to hike near London?

When I got home I started out joining some walking groups, because I had no idea what I was doing. Once I built up my confidence I started going out alone. Day trips from London turned into weekend trips further away. Over the years I have moved to South Devon for a few months to tackle parts of the South West Coast Path, and Yorkshire for seven months to hike in some of the most beautiful landscape in the country.

But I'm really based in London. This is my home. I also don't have a car as I sold it to buy a Vespa when I got home from backpacking (then it was stolen and that was that). When I'm not physio-ing, I spend my free time catching a train out of the city for a good old countryside walk, and in answer to my earlier question. Yes, it turns out there are hikes near London. So many incredible hikes, and I want to share them all with you.

A bit about the walks.

The walks I have chosen for this book are some of my favourite ones, and I have done them all multiple times.

My routes cover the South Downs National Park, The Chilterns National Landscape, The Surrey Hills National Landscape, The Kent Downs National Landscape, The High Weald National Landscape and the South East Coast Path. All these National Landscapes were formally 'Areas of Outstanding National Beauty' (AONBs). We have 34 of them in England and four surrounding London (you could argue there are some more depending on how far out you travel). As of 22 November 2023, all AONBs were renamed 'National Landscapes' to reflect the importance of them.

What the name or designation means is that it's a protected landscape, as per the Countryside and Rights of Way Act 2000, on par with National Parks, with teams working to protect and enhance the natural beauty. AONBs first came about after the Second World War as a way to protect the areas, during increasing demand for new development.

What you need to know:

- Every single one of my walks can be reached using public transport from, and back to London. They all start at a train station, and all bar one finishes at a train station too (the other finishes at a bus stop). Journey times range from 30 min to 1h45min.

- If you prefer to use a car, you can do that too! I have provided parking information in each guide and how to adapt the walk if needed. Although I would suggest you always check on the current available parking online, before setting out. I have provided the post codes, however, these show you the area boundary and not the specific location of the car park. So I would suggest Googling the car park name which I have provided.

- There are walks in here for almost all ability levels. Easy walks, very challenging walks and everything in-between. Whilst I do discuss terrain and what you can expect to find, I don't specifically cover wheelchair accessible walks.

- The distances of these walks range from 3.5 miles to 14 miles, and where there is an option to shorten a walk I have explained how to do so.

- For the most part these walks can be done any time of year, however, in each individual guide I will tell you when I think is the best time and if required, which times to avoid.

- I have provided information on amenities, where to eat, where the pubs are etc.
- All route descriptions are accurate at the time of writing, however, nature is nature and likes to change sometimes. Sometimes parts of trails can be closed off, in which case there should be a diversion with signs in place.

Distance tracking

The mileages for all these walks have been recorded station to station, and there can be slight variations in the distance and elevation due to GPS discrepancies, particularly if you are without signal or under lots of tree cover. I tracked all the routes using three different tracking methods and they all say something a little different. Only a little different though, so it's not an issue.

Getting there

Check the trains when planning which day you want to do the walks, as there are sometimes rail replacement works. This is usually on weekends. You will also find that some route journey times vary between weekend and weekday (weekdays are usually faster).

For the cheapest train tickets, travel off-peak. All weekends are off-peak, and during a weekday it varies by route, usually after about 10am. I would also recommend getting a railcard, which gives you 1/3 off rail travel.

AllTrails

On the directory pages for each section you will find a QR code. Scan the code with your mobile device, and you will be taken directly to AllTrails app to find maps designed personally by Zoe. You can download and use the AllTrails app for free.

If you ever have any trouble accessing the QR codes, you can find all the maps directly on Zoe's AllTrails account, just search Zoe Tehrani under members on AllTrails and go to 'Saved Lists'.

Safety and hiking etiquette.

- Always tell someone where you are going and set a time to check in for when you expect to finish.
- Be mindful of how many daylight hours there are vs the length of the walk. During winter, for the longer walks, you will want to leave early to ensure you have enough time to finish before the sun sets.
- If you have no signal and need to call for help, you might still be able to contact 999, as your phone will try to connect to any available network. Not just your phone provider. Another option is to send a text, which requires less bandwidth and signal. You would need to register for this service by texting 'register' to 999.
- Make sure you have the appropriate gear for the hike (more on this later), and a first aid kit.
- Linking to the above, check the weather before heading out. I think it goes without saying to avoid big storms.
- Take your phone and have a power bank just in case.
- If you are fairly new to hiking, don't hike out of your ability. What I mean by this is, build yourself up. Start with easy walks and as you get fitter and more experienced go for the bigger or more remote ones.
- If you find yourself in a field with cows, give them a wide berth. Most of the time they are chill, but there are exceptions. I always have a scan of every field I enter, and if there are cows, I keep to the edge even if it means walking off trail, and have my escape route planned.
- If you find yourself walking on a country road, stay alert (don't wear earphones), keep to the edge. Best to be on the side of oncoming traffic, but when going around corners be on the outer edge.
- Some of the walks feature chalk cliffs, which can be unstable. So keep away from the edges when on top, and don't walk directly under them when below.
- Know the route. Study it before leaving so you know roughly what you will be doing, where you can get food or water if it's needed, or where you can finish the walk early. I have also provided this information in the guides. Have a map downloaded and available for use offline, or as a printed copy. Particularly important if parts of the trail are closed off or have become inaccessible and you need to find an alternate route.
- If you get lost out there, don't panic. South East England isn't the wilderness.
- After a walk, check your body for ticks, particularly if you have been walking in long grass/overgrowth/woodland areas. I never used to check... until one got me.
- Leave no trace. Take all your rubbish with you, and don't stomp through flowers. Basically leave it like you were never there.
- When on a hill, the person walking uphill has the right of way. However, Large groups should give way to small groups.

What to wear.

Proper hiking gear can be expensive, but it has been specifically designed to work with the elements, which is why it's really worth investing if you plan to do a lot of hiking all year around.

You don't need every bit of kit out there, but there are a few staples I recommend everyone has.

For the walks in this book, you aren't far out in the wilderness, and if it's a heatwave summer, some of the essential items aren't going to be needed yet. The main thing I recommend you start with is hiking boots/shoes with good grip. The rest of the essentials are to cover you for all year round hiking, but won't necessarily be needed for every hike.

If it's in-between weather, so not hot, but not quite in the depths of winter, items such as jackets, won't necessarily be needed throughout a hike, but you should have them on you. It will get colder once you stop for breaks, and it's England so rain could come at any moment.

For your base layer (bottoms/top), the main thing is nothing that chafes (no denim), and for your top half I would avoid cotton as it tends to not be good at moisture wicking. Wool and synthetic are recommended instead, which wicks the sweat away from your body and evaporates.

Fancy gear isn't essential, but it will just make you more comfortable. I tend to wear gym shorts or leggings and then a proper hiking top.

Absolute Essentials

If you are starting from scratch, this is what you should get first:
- Hiking boots.
- Waterproof hiking jacket/trousers.
- Insulated jacket.
- Fleece.
- Hat/gloves.

Additional recommended equipment

Once you have got the absolute essentials, this is what I recommend investing in next:
- Hiking backpack + waterproof cover – some backpacks come with a cover, otherwise you can just buy one separately. They aren't very expensive.
- Hiking socks. Good hiking socks are designed to help prevent blisters and allow your feet to breathe.
- Moisture wicking top – synthetic or merino wool. Not cotton.
- Gaiters – I only started wearing these more recently, and they have been a game changer.
- Sun hat.
- Sunglasses.

Day hike packing list

What you pack can mean the difference between a great day out and a miserable existence. Trust me, I have learnt the hard way.

What you should pack for every day hike:

Essentials:
- Food/snacks +/- insulated food flask. Good for summer to keep your food fresh.
- Water.
- First aid kit including emergency shelter, tick remover, and whistle.
- Light/headtorch.
- Pocket tissues.
- Mini rubbish bag.
- Hand sanitiser.
- Lip balm (probably not essential, but I always bring some).
- Power bank for phone.
- Navigation system (map).
- Extra layers.

Occasional essentials:
What you will need on some day hikes depending on weather, time of year, hike location and type.
- Sunscreen.
- Sunglasses/sun hat.
- Gaiters.
- Waterproof backpack cover (although mine lives in my bag, so it's always with me anyway).
- Insect repellant.
- If coming by car: Spare shoes, socks, clothes. Also something to put your boots on to protect your car from the mud.

PUBLIC TRANSPORT

Getting into the South Downs from London will take anywhere from just under 1h to about 1h 30min, and these are the routes used:

London Waterloo – South Western Railway.

Clapham Junction – South Western Railway, Southern Railway.

London Victoria – Southern Railway.

London Bridge – Thameslink.

WALK 1
Black Down Temple of the Winds
9 miles

WALK 2
Hassocks to Lewes via Ditchling Beacon
10 miles

WALK 3
Amberley to Bignor Hill
8.5 miles

WALK 4
Hassocks to Devil's Dyke
9.5 miles

WALK 5
Lewes circular via Southease
11.5 miles

WALK 6
Southease to Seaford via Alfriston
14.5 miles

WALK 7
Amberley to Arundel
6 miles

SOUTH DOWNS NATIONAL PARK

The South Downs are my favourite place to come for a walk from London. Vast panoramic views almost wherever you go, endless rolling hills, views out to the sea. It's just so open and spacious, which is just what you need coming from London. Let's also not forget the white chalk cliffy coastline, rivers, ancient woodland and historic market towns and villages. I always feel such peace when I'm down here.

Covering over 1000 square miles, The South Downs is England's newest National Park, designated in March 2010. Located south of London, below the Surrey Hills and High Weald, through the counties of Hampshire, West Sussex and East Sussex.

Somewhere like here, there has to be a long distance walking trail. Of course there is. The South Downs Way. It's a 100-mile-long trail running from Winchester on the far west side to Eastbourne on the far east side.

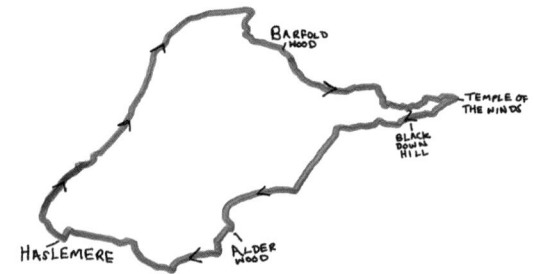

WALK 1

Black Down Temple of the Winds

Temple of the Winds is a viewpoint at the top of Black Down Hill, with arguably the best view across the South Downs National Park.

Before doing the walk for the first time, I had read about how it has the best view across the South Downs, and to be honest, I was a little sceptical. The photos I saw were alright, not mind-blowing. I figured people just said that as clickbait.

Let me tell you, when I got up there I was lost for words, granted, I had no one with me to say any words to in any case, so who knows.

The views are beyond amazing, and I wouldn't hesitate to say maybe the best I have seen on a walk down in this part of England. Better than Leith Hill and Box Hill which are the well known ones. Photos do not do it justice in any way.

You would think to continue straight through the open gate. Don't do that...

WHAT TO EXPECT

Starting in the quaint village of Haslemere, there is a bit of road before you take a trail steeply uphill around the back of houses. It's then a big downhill through a mass of woods, past quaint houses, and then more woods. It gets quite rugged here with wooden plank bridges and narrow off-piste trails.

This is followed by some open fields surrounded by thick trees and the occasional enviable house poking out through them. It's then more woods, which can be jungle-like at times, and then a short bit of road to reach the hill. The big hill. It's very steep and very rugged, but once you reach the top it will be worth it. This is Black Down Hill, the star of the walk.

Around the top of Black Down Hill, you will be surrounded by heather and pine trees, with views for miles. At 280m above sea level, Black Down Hill is the fourth highest hill in South East England. Not settling for being fourth, it is in fact the highest in the South Downs.

FUN FACT:

Apparently, Lord Tennyson (an English poet from the 19th Century) used to walk around the area wrapped in his cloak, and would sit up at Temple of the Winds getting inspiration for his poetry. There is a QR code at Temple of the Winds which will give you some info.

To walk back it's a nice descent now on the other side, through all the trees, to reach a road. This will lead you back to where you were earlier on in the walk and from here you can retrace your steps back (don't worry, I've given directions in the route description if you aren't sure).

Oh, and another thing, for this walk you will go between two counties, with Haslemere being in Surrey and Black Down and Temple of the Winds being in Sussex.

DIRECTORY

LOGISTICS:

Start/Finish: Haslemere Station, Surrey.
Difficulty: Moderate.
Type: Circular.
Route Distance: 9 miles/14km.
Time: 3–4h.

HOW TO GET THERE:

There are direct trains to Haslemere from London Waterloo and Clapham Junction, South Western Railway. Journey time 50 min to 1h.

COMING BY CAR:

Chestnut Avenue Car Park in Haslemere, GU27 2AB, RingGo App payment. Or free parking (at the time of writing) on Tennyson's Lane at Black Down Hill, GU27 3BJ. If you park here, it will be a different walk. Once you get to the hilltop, you can freestyle.

ELEVATION GAIN:

610m/2000ft.

TERRAIN:

Dirt trail, lots of mud, grass trail, some road, stiles.

DOG FRIENDLY:

Yes, with some precautions. Some livestock about. On Black Down Hill must be on a lead. The stiles all have doggy holes.

PHONE SIGNAL:

Yes.

PUBLIC TOILETS:

Yes. At the station only.

IDEAL TIME OF YEAR:

Around late August to see the heather in bloom, or autumn for the seasonal tree colours.

OPTION TO SHORTEN THE WALK:

Only if coming by car. Park at Tennyson's Lane and just walk around the top of Black Down hill.

WHERE TO EAT?

All options are in Haslemere. Nothing along the route.

CAFE AND COFFEE:

Haslemere

- The Courtyard Cafe (dogs outside only).
- Hemingways of Haslemere (dogs outside only).
- Heidi (dog friendly).

PUB:

Haslemere

- The White Horse (dog friendly).

FOR SUPPLIES:

Waitrose.

TIPS/OTHER THINGS TO KNOW

- Lots of sitting benches at the top of Black Down Hill.
- Can get very muddy after rain.
- Hiking boots recommended.

ROUTE DESCRIPTION

When you exit the station, take a left and follow the main road around and past the town. A word of advice, after leaving the station, walk on the other side of the road. The pavement on this side ends where there is a blind bend in the road.

Once you pass the main part of town, look out for a small trail next to one of the houses on the right, leading uphill, and take it.

This section is quite narrow, a bit muddy and quite steep. It takes you up a dirt trail, and then steps, until you reach the road.

At the road, cross it to pick up the trail on the other side.

When you reach the next road, the trail picks up again to the left, then the first right. There is a signpost here to guide you.

The trail continues through more bushes, and then trees, as it begins to take you downhill.

Out of the trees, you will be on a sort of driveway type road. Continue straight down past some houses to get to the next road with a pond on the other side.

Walk off-piste through the woods

Now, this is where things get fun. If you turn left on the road, you would think to continue straight through the open gate. Don't do that. Instead, you should see a wooden signpost just before it on the right. Follow that. It will take you into the trees and onto a very off-piste style trail.

Keep going, and you will reach another wooden signpost guiding you to the right, and along a long wooden plank, then up a small hill. Note: This might be a bit slippy if it's been raining. So be careful.

Once you reach the top, go left. This is where it can get particularly muddy.

My first time here, I passed a couple of people along here walking their dogs, and one woman exclaimed how muddy it was. Yes it was. Despite the fact that I wear waterproof hiking boots, I can't help but always do the mud dance.

Anyway, keep going to reach the gate which takes you into an open field.

Walk through the fields

Follow the trail through the field. There will probably be cows in here. Each time I've done this walk I've ended up skirting around the edge, as the cows like to sit on the trail. It's quite boggy around the edge, and a bit cobwebby.

Out of the gate on the other side, you will walk past a cute brick house, then at the road, pick up the trail on the other side with the wooden signpost.

The next bit of the trail is super narrow between the fence and the bushes. It will lead you through a gate at the end with a horse field in front.

At the horses, turn left to walk along the wide grassy trail.

Towards the end of this trail, you might think it's a dead end, but as you get closer to the fence, you will see you can zigzag through it.

Walk back into the woods

Follow the trail as it takes you downhill, then left into the woods again. This next bit is nice and off-piste, as it takes you further down with a sharp right bend at the wooden post.

You will then see the main trail below, and might wonder where I have taken you, as it's a steep drop to get onto it. Don't panic. If you walk to the right, you will be led down to it more safely. When you get down there, turn left. This is another very muddy section.

At the end of this trail, go straight across the road and up a short steep hill, then turn right. There are a couple of wooden signposts along this way to guide you.

Walk along some more muddiness towards the light, and out of the woods. The trail becomes grassy as it takes you to the left, with a lovely view across the rooftops to the hills of the South Downs on the right.

At the next signpost, continue straight and then into some more woodland.

At the junction with a big bush, you can take either trail. Left is more sensible. If you follow this, then take a right at the next junction, and you will reach a road bend with a house.

I prefer the right. Right feels more jungle-like.

If you take the right, then at the next junction go left, and then left again at the next junction. The further you go into this, the more wild it becomes. You will eventually reach that same road bend as above.

At the road, turn left to walk along it, with a lovely view across the hills to the right. Whoever lives in the house here is very lucky with that view.

You are now quite close to Temple of the Winds, but you aren't very high up. Which can only mean one thing. A steep uphill.

This track will curve to the left and uphill to reach the road. Here you will get an even better view across the South Downs. A taste of what is about to come.

Walk up to Temple of the Winds

At the road, to the right and a bit further along is a trail leading uphill to the left. Walk up this hill, then at the National Trust sign, take the trail to the left.

This is where the uphill slog begins. Steep and breathy.

As you near the top, you will walk through a gate, then continue up a little more.

As you continue up, things become a bit less specific when it comes to trails. If you stick to the right, you should reach a wooden bench with a brilliant view across the South Downs.

Walk past the bench, keeping to the right trail. This will guide you to a stone curved bench. This is Temple of the Winds, with the most breathtaking view out across the South Downs.

A good lunch spot.

Walk across the top of Black Down Hill

Now you will walk across the top of Black Down Hill. You can freestyle up here, but I will describe to you the route which takes you across and down the other side.

Continue past the stone bench, up the trail across the tree roots.

At the junction, take the right, then when you reach the Temple of the Winds sign, take the main obvious trail to the right.

When you reach the pond, turn onto the trail on the left.

Walk a short way up this trail, and you will be surrounded by heather, and a wonderful view ahead.

Follow the view to reach the slightly more civilised trail on the other side.

Black Down western viewpoint

At this main trail, turn right. You will be walking with a gorgeous view to the left, and a bit further along, another wooden viewpoint bench.

Continue to walk along the trail, and you will reach yet another viewpoint bench known as the Black Down Western Viewpoint.

Walk off-piste…or not

At the Blackdown western viewpoint, you can stay on the main trail, or go off-piste. I like the off-piste, engulfed in heather.

If you want to follow the main trail, keep going along it. Then either take the first left, then a left at the next junction or you can take the second left and stay on that trail.

For the off-piste route, if sitting on the bench, the trail is diagonal right, at about 1 o'clock.

This will take you along a very narrow trail amongst the heather. Possibly a bit scratchy if you aren't wearing trousers.

Follow this trail as it curves slightly to the right.

At the junction, take the diagonal left, then continue straight at the next junction.

When you reach the main path, turn left. If you took the main trail from the Black Down viewpoint, you should end up here as well.

Walk off Black Down Hill

At any junctions, stay straight, and you should reach a big gate.

Go straight through the gate, and along more dirt trail to reach another junction. You can go either way here as both join up later on.

If you take the left, then at the next junction, turn right and you will reach a gate.

If you take the right, continue to the end to reach the gate.

There are actually two gates here. If you took the right trail, you might end up at the wrong gate. The gate you want is further to the left.

Through the gate, you will make a steep decline through the trees, down Black Down Hill. At the bottom, the trail curves to the left to take you through a gate and into a field.

Now walk straight across the field, along a wide grass trail, with a view to a manor house poking out of the trees ahead.

At the end of the field, through the gate, go left. This will take you further downhill with a wonderful view of the bushy trees all around.

When you reach the bottom, turn left to walk through a gate, and follow the trail down to the road.

Turn right on the road, and follow it past another gorgeous enviable home, to reach the junction you were at earlier on in the walk. That bit where you took the first off-piste.

Walk back to Haslemere

You can now retrace your steps back to the start. If you're not sure though, this is how it goes:

Turn right before the house and continue up the road to reach the trail. There is a fork here. You need to take the left one. You now have a steep uphill through the woods.

When you reach the road, turn left then almost immediately right.

Follow the trail, then cross straight over the next road, and you will reach those steps to take you down to Haslemere. When you reach the main road, turn left. This will lead you past the town, and then to the station.

WALK 2

Hassocks to Lewes via Ditchling Beacon

You often have to work hard to get amazing views. Not on this one. Well, you have to work a little bit. But only a little. This is mostly a ridge walk with views all around you of the South Downs National Park and the vale down below. You even get a view out to sea. But you have to get up to the ridge first.

One thing I love about this walk is the simplicity of it. Up on the ridge, not much navigation is needed, and you can just walk. Walk and admire the views.

FUN FACT:
Ditchling Beacon, at 248m high, is the highest point in East Sussex, and the third highest in the South Downs.

> *Then you
> go up.
> Steeply up.*

WHAT TO EXPECT

The walk starts out relatively flat alongside some woodland. Followed by a bit of navigation across the road and a sports green to reach the foot of the South Downs.

Then you go up. Steeply up. The views start here. The uphill takes some of your breath away, but when you see the view, it will take the rest.

You will pass by the Jack and Jill windmills, and then reach the South Downs Way, which you follow for the next 5 miles or so, along the ridge, with incredible views the entire way.

The trail undulates up here, with a few cows and sheep, possibly a lot of wind, and Ditchling Beacon, an Iron Age hill fort.

At the 7 mile mark, you will start the descent to Lewes, a really charming medieval town. Once you reach the town, it's still about a 20min walk to reach the station, which sounds like a pain, but it's not so bad as you pass by a mixture of Tudor buildings and colourful house facades.

DIRECTORY

LOGISTICS:

Start/Finish: Hassocks Station, Sussex. Lewes Station, East Sussex.
Difficulty: Easy/Moderate.
Type: Point to point.
Route Distance: 10 miles/16 km.
Time: 3–4h.

HOW TO GET THERE:

Direct trains from London Victoria to Hassocks and Lewes, but you will have to buy two tickets as they are not fully on the same route.

They follow the same route until Haywards Heath then change direction, so buy a return ticket to Hassocks, and a single ticket from Lewes to Haywards Heath, then your return ticket will cover the remainder of the journey. Journey times are about an hour give or take a bit.

COMING BY CAR:

I would suggest parking in the car park at Ditchling Beacon, BN6 8XD, then freestyling along the ridge. It's free for National Trust Members or PaybyPhone app.

ELEVATION GAIN:

354m/1161ft.

TERRAIN:

Dirt trails, some mud, gravel trails, grass, a bit of road. No stiles.

DOG FRIENDLY:

There are a few sheep and cows roaming around, there's not a lot of shelter when walking along the top, but otherwise, yes.

PHONE SIGNAL:

Yes.

PUBLIC TOILETS:

Yes, at both stations.

IDEAL TIME OF YEAR:

Any time of year is good for this one. I would just avoid weather extremes as it's quite exposed.

OPTION TO SHORTEN THE WALK:

Only if walking partway and turning back. There is the 79 bus at Ditchling Beacon, but it's seasonal hours and goes to Brighton.

WHERE TO EAT?

There's a couple of seasonal options along the route, Hassocks has a few options, and Lewes is full of good places. Here are some suggestions.

CAFE AND COFFEE:

Hassocks

- Green Folk Kitchen (dog friendly).
- Purple Carrot in Hassocks (dog friendly).

On the walk

- 1.5 miles: The Pink Pit Stop coffee truck at the windmill.
- 4 miles: ice cream truck at Ditchling Beacon (both seasonal hours).

Lewes

- The Sip (dog friendly).
- Carafe Coffee Roasters (dog friendly).

PUB:

Hassocks

• The Hassocks (dog friendly).

Lewes

• Rights of Man (dog friendly).

FOR SUPPLIES:

Sainsbury's Local in Hassocks. Morrisons and Waitrose in Lewes.

TIPS/OTHER THINGS TO KNOW

• It will probably be a bit busy around the Ditchling Beacon area, but I find the rest of the route not that busy.

• Hiking boots recommended.

• Most of the route isn't too muddy, except the horsey area near Lewes. That's very muddy.

*Make sure to look
back for the most
incredible view*

ROUTE DESCRIPTION

Out of the station, walk down the road to the right, and you will see a sign for the South Downs on a wall, pointing down a side path. Take it.

At the main road, turn right, and just before the bridge there will be another South Downs sign pointing left to some steps. Take these steps.

Continue along this path for about a mile, ignoring the paths that lead off it. You will mostly be enclosed by bush and tree cover, skirting along the edge of Butcher's Wood and Lag Wood, before reaching an opening with fields to your left and a view of the South Downs up ahead. A nice big hill, which you will have to walk up soon.

When you reach the road, turn left, then cross the road to go through a gate into a big sports field. Head to the car park on the right, and out the other side, then directly across the road you should see a South Downs sign. Follow it between the houses, and then up a very steep hill.

The hill and Clayton windmills

When you reach the open field, there is signage pointing in lots of directions. Basically, just walk up the hill. It's a steep and breathy uphill. Make sure to look back for the most incredible view though when you get up there. It feels like you can see the whole world.

Continue walking up, keeping the fence to your right, and you should see a white windmill up ahead. That is Jill. Then just behind her you should see Jack. Head towards them.

Facts about Jill

Built in 1821, she originally lived in Brighton. Then in 1852 was moved to Clayton by horses. She stopped working in the early 1900's, has suffered damage by storms, and decades later was restored to working order. When the wind is blowing enough she is able to produce stoneground wholemeal flour (from local organic wheat), which you can buy if you visit her.

Facts about Jack

Jack is one of the few male mills in England, and he stopped working in the early 1900's. That's all.

The South Downs Way

Go through the gate onto a path just next to the windmills, and this will lead you to a road.

Go left here, and shortly after you will see the South Downs Way sign at the junction. If you look back when walking along here, you will get a better view of Jack.

Hassocks to Lewes via Ditchling Beacon

Welcome to the South Downs Way.

Turn left here through a gate, and for the rest of the way, the route is well signposted. For now, just follow the South Downs Way signs. You are going to be walking in this direction up here now for about 5ish miles.

As you continue along this trail, if you take a look to the right, you will get a glimpse of the sea and a wind farm in the distance.

You will be on an enclosed trail for a moment, before reaching the open fields, with spectacular views of the undulating hills ahead, and those far reaching views to the left. I've squinted really hard, trying to see London. You can't see London.

Following the ridge, you may see some sheep or cows. I have a thing about cows in fields. A phobia, if you will.

Ditchling Beacon

When you reach Ditchling Beacon, you will have a wonderful view down the steep hill ahead, and far out into the distance. This area will be a little busier.

Apart from there being a car park, the road through here is a popular cycling route, and actually part of the London to Brighton cycle challenge.

On the gate here, there is a QR code to scan which will give you a bit of history of the area.

The route continues past Ditchling Beacon across the undulating hilltop, with those rolling hills ahead and to the right, and the 'world' to the left. Mostly on grass, with a bit of gravel path thrown in.

When you reach a hairpin bend, take the right one.

Leave the South Downs Way

So far, you will have been walking in a straight direction, following the South Downs Way. You will know it's time to leave the South Downs Way when the sign directs you down a trail to the right.

Instead, go through the gate, and continue straight, which will take you towards Lewes. There is also a sign here pointing to Lewes.

When you reach the grass trail split, take the right one, and follow it all the way into the woods. It's all downhill now.

Walk to Lewes

When you reach the horsey area (the race course), do a little zigzag when you see an information board to the right (turn right to the information board, then left), which will lead you onto the road.

Keep going straight and you will be led onto a very muddy trail. This must be for the horses.

Keep following this all the way down (don't worry, it's not mud the whole way), to reach the road and Lewes.

To reach the station, continue straight across the road, and keep going, passing by some Tudor buildings, and pastel coloured houses to reach the high street and town centre.

Then it's a right turn on station road, to reach the, you guessed it, station.

I might suggest instead taking a right on Watergate Lane a bit before. It's a narrow downhill alley between the old buildings. Very quaint.

WALK 3

Amberley to Bignor Hill

This walk takes you up to the top of Bignor Hill, with the most incredible views down into the Arun Valley and across the rolling hills of the South Downs. I thought I saw an eagle up here once. I wasn't sure, as I don't know birds. So I looked it up and discovered that two white-tailed eagles were released into the South Downs in 2020 as part of a rewilding project. This is the area they like to hang out. I did get a photo, and it turns out it's a black or red kite. The jury is still out on which one.

But there is something else that makes this walk particularly special. Houghton Forest. When I came out and tried this walk for the first time, the forest was an afterthought. I had actually planned to skirt around the edge of it. I wasn't in a forest mood. But when I arrived, I was mesmerised by what I saw. I had to go in.

Dense fairytale-like forest, with looming trees, plants I'd never seen before. I felt like I was in another world.

There is definitely a bit of a spooky-lost-in-the-woods vibe.

WHAT TO EXPECT

The walk starts out along the River Arun, before you head up the big hill to reach the Houghton Forest, roughly 2 miles in. There is one very nasty road crossing. You will need to be on alert and catch a moment to cross, then run.

It's then about 1 mile through the deepest part of the forest, along an off-piste type trail. There is definitely a bit of a spooky-lost-in-the-woods vibe, no phone signal, and absolute silence interrupted occasionally by rustling in the surrounding abyss. The route through is easy to follow though.

FUN FACT:
Celtic legend has it that there was once a dragon's lair on top of Bignor Hill.

After the forest, you will head to Bignor Hill, where all the views are, along with lots of birds. Bignor Hill is around the halfway mark, or slightly over. It's then a downhill, then another uphill to reach the forest again, and from there, you retrace your steps back to Amberley.

DIRECTORY

LOGISTICS:

Start/Finish: Amberley Station, West Sussex.
Difficulty: Easy/moderate.
Type: Circular.
Route Distance: 8.5miles/13.5km.
Time: 3–4h.

HOW TO GET THERE:

Direct trains from London Victoria to Amberley on Southern Railway. Journey time 1h 23min.

COMING BY CAR:

Free parking at Bignor Hill (S Downs Way parking) RH20 1PH. It's right next to the trail that takes you up the hill. The route description takes you through it, so you can follow from there. I would suggest not walking to Amberley, and to instead circle back through the forest. That would make this a 5 mile walk.

ELEVATION GAIN:

About 449m/1473ft.

TERRAIN:

Grass, dirt trail, chalk trail, possible mud, road. No stiles.

DOG FRIENDLY:

Yes. There is livestock, but I've only seen them in fenced away fields. Main thing is caution with the road crossing.

PHONE SIGNAL:

None through the bulk of the woods. Yes for the rest of the route.

PUBLIC TOILETS:

No.

IDEAL TIME OF YEAR:

Autumn is wonderful for the colourful leaves in the forest.

OPTION TO SHORTEN THE WALK:

It's possible, but you would miss out on something. An option would be to skip the forest and just walk to Bignor Hill and back. It's easy to follow, as when you reach the forest, don't go in, but instead just follow the South Downs Way signs and this will lead you to Bignor Hill. This will be a 7.5 mile walk.

WHERE TO EAT?

Only in Amberley. Nothing along the route.

CAFE AND COFFEE:

Riverside Tea Rooms (dog friendly).

PUB:

The Bridge Inn (dog friendly).

FOR SUPPLIES:

None.

TIPS/OTHER THINGS TO KNOW

- Whilst I felt safe in the woods, I can see how some might get a bit nervous in there. So if you think that might be you, then I'd skip the forest section of the walk as described above.
- Hiking boots recommended.
- You won't actually see the main village of Amberley, interestingly, it's a good 25min walk away from the station in the opposite direction.
- If you fancy doing something a bit different, you can hire an e-bike, next to the bridge in Amberley. This whole route can pretty much be done on a bike. I did take a couple of trails which aren't for bikes, but there are alternate ones you can take to complete the route. I've rented an e-bike from there before and highly recommend it. They can download a route for you on Strava to follow, and will attach your phone to the bike. Tell them you want to do Bignor Hill and Houghton Forest, and they will get the bike route map up for you.

Walking through the forest, it's pure silence.

ROUTE DESCRIPTION

Out of the station, turn left to walk to the main road, then left again towards the bridge.

You now have two route options along the river.

Option 1: Turn right at the first turning and walk to the river, then follow it to reach the bridge, then cross over and turn right to continue along the river.

Option 2: Walk over the bridge past the pub, then turn right, and continue along the river past the second bridge.

Whichever way you take, continue now past the (second) bridge with the river to your right, then take the first left turn at the South Downs Way sign. You are going to follow this sign all the way to the forest now.

The big hill you can see ahead. That's where you are heading. It looks a bit scary, but it's not so bad when you are making your way up.

Following this trail, it will do a right then left bend to reach a road. This is a nice road, don't worry.

Cross straight over the road, and you'll now start to make your way up the hill. Just a warning, the terrain can be a bit slippy here.

Stay on this main trail as it does a few curves, to reach the road. This is the nasty road I talked about earlier. It's a well used national speed limit road, however, there will be gaps where you can cross. Just make sure you are quick.

Once across, follow the South Downs Way sign to the right, then take the trail on the left.

Now follow this trail, and it will lead you to the forest on a gentle uphill.

Just before the forest is a junction. Take the right diagonal (at 2 o'clock) following the South Downs Way sign.

If you are planning to skip the forest and just head to Bignor Hill, then stay on the trail. To enter the forest, take a left turn very shortly after the junction to enter it.

Houghton Forest

Now, when you get in, follow this trail, then a very short way along, look out for a very missable trail to the left. This will take you deeper into the forest.

You are now going to follow this trail for about 1 mile, all the way to the end. When I say end, I mean the official looking trail. You are currently on an off-piste trail.

It takes you through a variety of huge trees, tight bush spaces, slightly more open spaces. Then when you reach a long stretch of wide grass, you will be nearing the end.

Walking through the forest, it's pure silence, broken up by rustling in the surrounding trees. I must admit, there have been moments where my imagination took me to wild beasts waiting to pounce. Then I started noticing pheasants. So it must be that.

When you reach the obvious trail at the end, turn right, then take the next left shortly after, along a grass trail lined with massive trees ahead. It gives me New Forest vibes. It's now another uphill, then when you reach the end, turn right, and follow this trail now for about 1 mile. This will lead you out of the forest towards Bignor Hill.

Bignor Hill

At the main junction, turn right, then a short way along you will reach a car parking area on the right, and a big signpost. Walk around the car park and you will see a trail running up a hill ahead.

That's where you go next. The summit of Bignor Hill.

This is the area, walking up the hill, where there are lots of birds. It's also where I saw the kite.

At the top (and as you make your way up) you will be surrounded by wonderful views across the South Downs and their undulating hills, down to the vale, and the dense forest you just walked through.

You are following the South Downs Way signs again, and actually, you can follow them all the way back to Amberley from this point. But I will guide you anyway, in case any signs go missing.

Walk back to Amberley

Over the hill, and down the other side, you will be led onto a trail between fence and bush, then take the left at the junction, and continue down some more. There is some potentially slippy trail here.

When you reach the bottom, turn to the right, to walk with the farm building to your left.

You are going to walk uphill again now. Sorry. But it does mean you get some more great views, particularly of the forest.

Now keep on this trail, and it will lead you back to where you entered the forest earlier. When you reach the junction past the forest, turn left, and this will lead you back to that road we don't like.

When you get there, walk to the right, then catch a safe moment to cross, to pick up the trail on the other side.

Now follow this, and it will lead you all the way down the hill. You will get a view of the bridge from here. So if in doubt, head towards that.

At the bottom, cross the road, and continue along the trail straight across.

Then through the gate, turn right, and this will lead you along the river all the way back to Amberley.

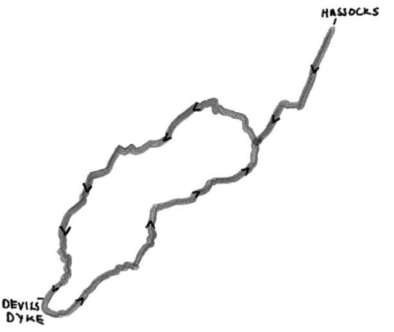

WALK · 4

Hassocks to Devil's Dyke

Devil's Dyke is a 100m deep V-shaped valley in the South Downs. It is in fact, the longest, deepest, and widest dry valley in the UK. During the Victorian era, there was a fun fair here, the remnants of which can still be seen today.

The first time I did this walk was after lockdown. I found myself in woods so tight that I almost had to crawl on my hands and knees. I accidentally walked through private land. I ran out of water halfway through, and considered knocking on some houses to get some. But with social distancing, that might not have been appropriate. I was so thirsty that I started to wonder if I should drink my wee. Although, I was so dehydrated that I didn't need a wee. I envisioned myself collapsing on one of the hills and shrivelling up, needing to be rescued. I then followed the big A-road to find a petrol station.

The walk itself though (apart from the woods and dehydration) was one of the most incredible I'd been on. The views are out of this world, the kind where photos don't do it justice, and walking around Devil's Dyke just takes your breath away.

I have learnt from my mistakes, and have come up with a much more sensible route. Sensible doesn't mean easy though. It's incredibly hilly all the way through.

Walk 4

There is another hill here which is the most bizarre hill I have encountered.

WHAT TO EXPECT

Lots of mud, the kind that sucks your boot off (it's happened to me), lots of cows, and lots of hills. You will basically be walking up and down hills all day.

The first couple of miles of the walk aren't very exciting, and there is a bit of road, and then you are faced with the first hill of the day. First through woods, and then out in the open with amazing views.

There is another hill here which is the most bizarre hill I have encountered (more on that later), and then you descend to cross over the A-road bridge (which is very loud). It's then straight back uphill.

Over the other side of the hill, you will get your first view of Devil's Dyke ahead, which you need to walk downhill then back up again to get to it.

There are a number of ways you can walk around Devil's Dyke, which I will explain in the route description. This marks the halfway point in the walk.

Then you make your way back to Hassocks, up another hill, and later on you will join up to one of the trails you got out here on. After which you make your way back the way you came, up and down a few more hills.

FUN FACT:

In true British style, there are a number of myths as to why it's called Devil's Dyke. The main one is that the Devil was digging a trench so that the sea would flood the churches, what happened next is up for debate. My favourite is that he stubbed his toe on a large rock and then abandoned the dig due to toe injuries.

Some say he was disturbed by a woman who lit a candle, others say roosters started crowing. Both of which made the Devil think daylight was coming so he abandoned the dig. He then apparently threw the last shovel of dirt over his shoulder which fell into the sea forming the Isle of Wight.

As fun as these stories are, science says that Devil's Dyke was created naturally during the last ice age.

DIRECTORY

LOGISTICS:

Start/Finish: Hassocks Station, Sussex.
Difficulty: Challenging.
Type: Circular.
Route Distance: 9.5 miles/15.5 km.
Time: 4–5 hours.

HOW TO GET THERE:

There are direct trains from London Victoria or London Bridge to Hassocks, Southern Railway, and Thameslink respectively. Journey time is about an hour.

COMING BY CAR:

You can park at Devil's Dyke National Trust car park BN1 8YL. It's free for members. You can follow the route description starting at Devil's Dyke, but once you reach the point where the route takes you to Hassocks, I would instead circle back.

ELEVATION GAIN:

666m/2185ft. That's nearly half of Ben Nevis.

TERRAIN:

Dirt trail, grass, lots of mud, little bit of road, lots of stiles and some steps.

DOG FRIENDLY:

To an extent. Dogs are allowed, and all the stiles have doggy holes. However, there is a lot of livestock, so they would need to be on a lead for a lot of it.

PHONE SIGNAL:

Patchy. A lot of it has no signal, particularly around the Devil's Dyke area, and other areas it's weak.

PUBLIC TOILETS:

No. But there are a few places to eat along the way which will have toilets.

IDEAL TIME OF YEAR:

I would say just avoid after heavy rain due to the mud.

OPTION TO SHORTEN THE WALK:

Kind of. Bus number 77 leaves from Devil's Dyke, but it takes you to Brighton, that would make this a 5 mile walk. Seasonal operating hours. Or if you go by car, you can then park at Devil's Dyke and freestyle around the area. Or do the circular as mentioned.

WHERE TO EAT?
CAFE AND COFFEE:

Hassocks

- Green Folk Kitchen (dog friendly).

On the walk

- 2.5 miles: Wayfield Park Farm Shop (dog friendly).
- 6 miles: The Wild Flower Cafe (dog friendly).

PUB:

Hassocks

- The Hassocks (dog friendly).

On the walk

- 5 miles: The Devil's Dyke Pub (dog friendly).

FOR SUPPLIES:
Sainsbury's Local in Hassocks.

TIPS/OTHER THINGS TO KNOW
- The Devil's Dyke area will likely be busy, but the rest of the route not so much.
- Wear hiking boots.

*Imagine you are
standing on a globe.
That's what it feels like.*

ROUTE DESCRIPTION

From Hassocks Station, you need to follow the road out of the car park, but not too far. The first turning is a small path behind the houses on the right. There should be a sign on the wall pointing to the South Downs.

When you reach the main road, turn right to walk towards the bridge. Just before the bridge there is a turning on the left on the other side of the road, leading you into some woods.

There are actually two paths next to each other. The one with the steps is the better one, so take that.

From here, the next mile is on a narrow, not very interesting trail between fence, woods, and bush. However, towards the end of it, things open up briefly and you get your first view of the South Downs hills ahead.

When you reach the road, cross over and turn right. If you look over the wall on the left you will see a really cool train tunnel. This is the Clayton Tunnel.

The first hill

Take the next left, and follow this road, then after about 160m there is a trail on the left. You start walking uphill now. It can be a little overgrown through here, and a bit scratchy through the bushes, but then it's less bush and more woodland. You will pass a sign saying Wolstonbury Hill, and then a big clay mud patch with these sort of tree stumps that look like stepping stones for someone with long legs.

At any junction, stay straight for the moment. This whole section is a bit under 1 mile, and then at a trail signpost turn right into a field with a big hill. It's the first right after the big junction you will have crossed. This is that bizarre hill I mentioned earlier. It's just so perfectly rounded. And a little unnerving, because you can't see what's over the hill, or to the sides. Imagine you are standing on a globe. That's what it feels like.

You can walk diagonally over it to the left, and you will reach a gate on the other side. Not being able to see what's over the hill, I choose to stick to the edge to walk around. Animals do live here sometimes. I've not seen them, but I've seen their trough.

I have been over the top of the hill once, and I was scared the whole time as you never actually reach the top and can never see what's just around the other side. But the views up there are incredible.

Through the gate on the other side of the hill, continue down the hill on a diagonal right, at about 2 o'clock, and then through a gap in the bushes and over two stiles.

Now head down to the right of the little cluster of houses you see at the bottom. You may see horses here. I've been cornered by these horses. They probably thought I had food, as they were trying to get into my backpack.

Being me, I feared for my life a little. I'm scared of big animals in fields.

At the bottom, go through the wooden gate, turn right, then take a left just before the track ahead. This will lead you through some bushes, over a stile, and then past the houses to reach the residential road.

Turn right, to then cross over the A-road bridge on the left.

The second hill

Continue straight a few meters past the bridge, then at the next junction, turn left. You'll go through a couple of gates, and past the farm shop, to enter a big field. This is a cow field. Luckily, the trail runs straight up along the edge, and further up you are hidden a bit from the cows by bushes.

Although, the cows sometimes hide in these bushes. I've had quite the shock walking along here, and suddenly finding myself faced with a cow.

As you walk up the hill, when you reach an open area where the left and right field connect, you should see a trail sign in the middle. Just continue straight up through the middle of the trees and bushes ahead.

At the top, go through the wooden gate, where you will see a New Timber Hill sign. Remember this point. When you walk back later in the walk, you will circle back and end up here.

You still want to walk in the direction of straight, but don't do it through the woods. Go up the little trail on the left into the field, and walk along the right edge of it. At the end of the field, go through the gate, and stay straight, and when you reach a grass trail junction at the big tree, take the right grass trail.

Now follow this wide obvious grass trail as it guides you around the top of the hill.

When you get to the other side, you will be greeted by a wonderful view of the rolling hills of the South Downs ahead, dropping down to the vale below.

When you reach two lone trees, leave this main trail to take the trail that runs between them. This will lead you along the side of the hill. Then when you reach a grass trail split, take the right one.

The hill you can see straight ahead now, with a valley down the other side, is Devil's Dyke. And yes, you need to walk down this hill to then walk up that one.

Walk towards Devil's Dyke

The grass trail will then turn to a narrow chalk and rock trail. Once you are on this trail, keep an eye out for a grass trail straight down the hill to the right. You wont notice it until you are right on it. But once you see it, it's obvious.

One time, when I was about to turn down on the trail, a cow suddenly appeared and started trotting towards me, mooing aggressively. I ran down that hill. It's very steep.

Down the hill, you should reach a road, which you cross straight over, and pick up the trail on the other side to the right.

A couple of meters along, look to the left and you should see a wooden bench. Walk to it, and walk down the hill here, to reach the obvious trail you see below.

When you get onto that trail, go straight across it to walk all the way to the bottom where there are bushes and a stile. Don't go over the stile. Trust me. I did it once. Instead, turn left to walk along the bottom.

When you reach the next stile and gate, go through it, then a short way along you will reach a path. You now want to do an upside down V. So basically, cross over the path and walk back, on the grassy trail on the other side of it. You will be walking now with a hill on your left, and bushes to your right.

Keep to the edge with the bushes, then through some bushes ahead, and then over a stile into the woods. When you reach the T-junction with a trail sign, turn left.

Follow this trail up through the woods to reach a wooden gate, and you will enter the bottom of Devil's Dyke.

Now, you have a few options here. This is what I suggest:

Option 1: Follow the left trail which will take you all along the top edge of the valley, then when you reach the other end, descend down into it and walk all the way though and you will end up back here. Then to continue on with this guide, go back along the trail on the left to reach the steps.

Option 2: The same as option one but in reverse. So walk through the middle of the valley, and up the other side, then turn left, and it will bring you back along the left trail, but don't come all the way back to this point. Turn off it when you see the steps ahead. When walking back on the left trail, there is a junction, which I will explain in option three.

Option 3: This takes you all the way around the whole perimeter of Devil's Dyke. For this one, I will describe the route below, as it's a bit more complex.

Walk around the top of Devil's Dyke

So, through this gate, walk to the right, and over the stile back into the woods. It's now more uphill, with a few steps thrown in. Keep following this dirt trail, then after about 450m you will reach a big junction. You want to do another backwards V here. Walk back now on the trail on the left so you are almost walking back on yourself.

There is yet again more uphill, but now the woods slowly start to dissipate and you get your first views looking down into the valley.

You are now going to stay on this main trail and through a couple of gates as you walk all the way to the other end, with the valley to your left.

Just before you reach the road at the end, you will reach a trail running straight across this one. Turn onto it to the left, then through another gate, and you will then get a perfect view looking straight down the middle of Devil's Dyke. (If you took option two through the middle of the valley then up, you should end up here).

If you'd like to go to the pub, it's up along the road.

Now continue following this trail around the other side, where the views just get better and better. The trail will become grassy before leading you onto a big obvious trail.

When you reach an opening with an animal trough to the left and trail sign to the right, you want to leave this main trail and take the less obvious trail through the bushes to the left.

Through there, a short way along, a more obvious but narrow trail will appear. You can now follow this to continue walking around the edge of Devil's Dyke.

As you near the other end, you will reach a trail split. Take the right one which leads to some steps into a field ahead.

Over the steps, continue straight to the other end of the field, then through a gate, and continue straight across the next field to reach some more steps, and the road.

Another hill

Across the road you should see a car parking area. Cross over to it, then along the path leading to Saddlescombe Farm.

When you reach the black gate on the left, go through it, and along the right trail. You are now following the South Downs Way for a bit, which will be signposted.

At the end of this trail (just a few meters), turn right, and then continue along the road.

Just to the right here is the Wild Flower Cafe if you want some refreshments.

Stay following this road right to the end and through a gate into the woods. Through the gate are two trails. Take the right one which leads you straight up a hill.

When you exit the trees, there will be a gate ahead. Don't go through it, but instead follow the trail to the left which will continue to take you uphill along the edge of the field.

This is a long uphill, but make sure to look back for incredible views.

When you reach the top and a gate, don't go through it, but turn left instead to continue along the perimeter of the field, staying straight at any junctions.

Now, there is another option up here. When you see a gate on the right, you can go through that and follow the trail diagonally down the hill, and it will get you back to the trail you walked up earlier in the walk. The advantage of that way is the views you will get. However, that field is full of cows, which is why I don't go that way. Unfortunately, my route has no views.

Staying straight (the way avoiding the cows), when you reach the very end, go past the bushes to a gate on the right. This is where you were earlier in the walk. The bit I told you to remember. From this point, you can retrace your steps all the way back to Hassocks. But I know that's easier said than done, so I will explain it to you.

Walk back to Hassocks

Through the gate, continue down the hill, first through the bushes, and then you reach that opening where two fields meet. The trail you want is to the left at 11 o'clock. Then continue all the way down to the gates and farm shop, then the bridge over the A-road.

Cross the bridge and turn right, then take the first left past the houses to reach the stile.

Over the stile, turn right to get to the gate with the field with horses.

In this field, head to the right and up the hill, yes more hills, I told you it was hilly, to reach the two stiles at the top.

In the next field, it's uphill some more to reach a gate. You are now at that bizarre perfectly domed hill.

Get to the other side of it to reach the gate. Through this gate, turn left, and it's now straight at any junction all the way down to reach the road.

At the road, turn right, then at the next road turn right with the Clayton train tunnel to your right. Cross over the road, to pick up the trail on the left.

Now follow this all the way to the end, about a mile, then when you reach the road, turn right, and take the little alleyway type walkway just ahead on the left, and you will reach the station.

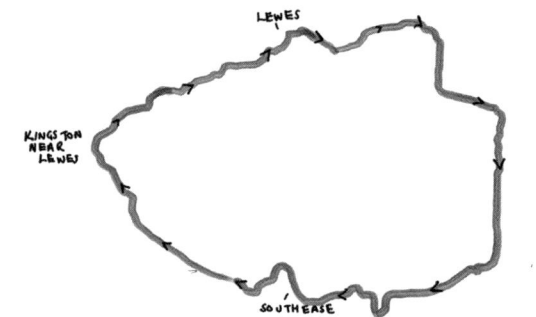

WALK 5

Lewes circular via Southease

The first time I did this walk, or a variation of it, I decided it was the best walk I had ever done. 360 degree views of the rolling hills of the South Downs. Patchwork fields of different shades of green, brown and yellow, a view out to the English Channel, which almost looked unreal. A perfectly sharp horizon of deep blue sea meeting the light blue sky. It was a glorious summer day, which probably helped.

I have since adapted it, making sure to include my favourite bits, but now making it a much more sensible length (that one was very long), and finishing this time back in Lewes for a pub.

This version of the walk takes you past Priory ruins dating back to the 11th century, across award winning wetland, and then along the South Downs Way for all the views.

Once up the top you will be rewarded with incredible views.

WHAT TO EXPECT

You will first walk through the Priory of St Pancras (also known as the Lewes Priory), for a bit of history. It's then a short bit of road to reach the Cockshut Stream Restoration Project which is the award winning wetland. If you are into your birds, there are lots of them around here. It can also get quite muddy in winter.

Next you head to Kingston near Lewes, which has a pub if you fancy, before you have to tackle a very steep and long(ish) uphill. You just have to remind yourself that this is the only hill, and once up the top you will be rewarded with incredible views.

FUN FACT:
The Lewes Priory of St Pancras is the first Cluniac Priory in Britain. It's also named after the same guy as London St Pancras, a Roman martyr called St Pancras.

From here it's easy as you follow the ridge for a few miles, then descend down, past a farm, and on to Southease where you can now just follow the River Ouse back to Lewes.

To the Pub

DIRECTORY

LOGISTICS:

Start/Finish: Lewes Station, East Sussex.
Difficulty: Moderate.
Type: Circular.
Route Distance: 11.5 miles/18.5 km.
Time: 4–5h.

HOW TO GET THERE:

Direct trains from London Victoria to Lewes on Southern Railway. Journey time 1h.

COMING BY CAR:

Mountfield Road car park, BN7 2UR. This is located near the Lewes Priory, so you can pick up the route description from there.

ELEVATION GAIN:

361m/1184ft.

TERRAIN:

Grass, mud, chalk, dirt, some road. No stiles.

DOG FRIENDLY:

Yes, but there are some loose cows about.

PHONE SIGNAL:

Yes.

PUBLIC TOILETS:

Yes, at Lewes Station. None along the route, unless you stop at the pub.

IDEAL TIME OF YEAR:

I would avoid if it is very windy due to being exposed on the ridge, otherwise, any time of year is fine. Also, just be aware that some parts will be quite muddy after rain.

OPTION TO SHORTEN THE WALK:

Yes. 8 miles in is Southease Station. This will take you back to Lewes.

WHERE TO EAT?

There are a couple of pubs along the route, and plenty of options in Lewes.

CAFE AND COFFEE:

Lewes

- Carafe Coffee Roasters (dog friendly).
- Ground Coffee (dog friendly).
- The Sip (dog friendly).

PUB:

On the walk

- 2 miles: The Juggs at Kingston, near Lewes (dog friendly).
- 7 miles: The Abergavenny Arms, near Southease (dog friendly).

FOR SUPPLIES:

Morrisons and Waitrose in Lewes.

TIPS/OTHER THINGS TO KNOW

- If it's very sunny, you might want sunglasses/a hat as you will be facing the sun for a portion of the walk.
- The end of the walk, back into Lewes, is unfortunately joined by the A27 and the noise that comes with it.
- Hiking boots recommended.

As you make your way up, make sure to look back at the views.

ROUTE DESCRIPTION

Out of the station, if you need supplies, the town centre is up the road to the right. For this walk, turn left out of the station, then at the end of the road, turn left again, then turn onto the path on the right just before the end.

Walk through to the end of the path, then turn right to walk with a wall to your right and field to your left. You should see a playground ahead. Walk towards it and through the gap to reach a big field with ruins. This is the Lewes Priory. As many as 100 monks lived here until its dissolution in the 16th Century. There's lots of information boards about, telling you about the history and the different buildings.

Walk to the wetland

You want to walk out the other side of the field, which you can do following the path to the left.

Out the other end, turn left on the road, then when you reach the end, turn right and follow it to walk under the A27. It will be very loud here.

Under the underpass, go through the gate on the right, and walk along the left side of the field.

Through another gate you will reach what looks like a big pond. This is part of the Cockshut Stream Restoration Project.

You can walk either way around it. I suggest going left, as you will get a wonderful view back towards Lewes and the white cliffs.

It might be a bit muddy around here by the way.

If you take the left, walk all the way around until you reach a bridge. Turn left at the bridge to walk through the gate and along a narrow dirt (and potentially very muddy) trail.

Walk to Kingston near Lewes

If you look ahead in the distance, you can see a big hill. That's where you are heading to.

When you reach the gate, go through it and turn left to follow the path.

At the end where it meets the road, cross over a bit to the right to walk past the cottage, and then pick up the trail past the timber framed house. This will lead you through a farm.

Through the farm, head through a gate which will be ahead to the left, then continue along the left side of the field.

Near the end, there will be a gate on the left. Now follow the trail through the gate and you will reach Kingston near Lewes.

If you cross straight over the road, and continue straight, you will pass the Juggs pub on the right.

Walk to the South Downs Way

Past the pub, continue straight along the road, passing the Kingston Parish Hall, and some quaint homes. The South Downs hills will be just ahead, and looks a bit scary from here.

Now, you can get onto a trail taking you up them if you stay straight, but I want to take you a slightly different way, which gives you a bit more views.

So, turn right to walk through the church, then out the other side turn left.

When you reach the road, turn right and continue all the way to the end. It's a big uphill along here, which is good. It gets some of it out of the way before the final push to the top. You might see a 'private road' sign walking along here. Don't worry about that.

When you reach the end, turn left. There is more than one left here. You want the one that leads straight towards the hill. If you have coffee with you, you might want to have some now.

Now, follow this trail, which is actually quite easy to begin with.

Through the gate, when you reach a junction, take the right uphill, following the restricted byway sign. This is where it starts to get steeper.

As you make your way up, make sure to look back at the views. And keep looking back at different points, as it changes as you go up. When you reach the top, continue straight and you should then see a big wide grass trail on the left. That's the South Downs Way.

Now turn left to follow it.

Follow the South Downs Way

You are now going to follow the South Downs Way all the way to Southease.

First you will be walking along the ridge, with a view down to the vale on one side, the undulating hills on the other, and the ridge as it stretches into the distance.

The views change as you continue along, keeping it interesting, and then Kingston near Lewes appears below around a corner.

You are going to be walking along this for a bit over 1 mile, through some gates, and the path will change from grass to more of a track.

The farm

When you reach the gate where the track turns to the right, follow it, then at the junction turn left, to follow the road. It's not a proper road. It's more of a road for the farm. It's a long one though. At first it's really cool, leading straight ahead with a view to the Seaford Head cliff on the coast way in the distance. It can get a little tedious though, when it's one straight line with seemingly no end. It does end though, after about 1 mile.

When you reach the end, go through the gate ahead, and now continue straight along the left edge of the field. This is all farmland. So it could be a bit muddy in places.

At the other end of the field, go through the gate, then cross the path and through the next gate and continue along the edge of the next field.

Along here you pass what I think is the Greenwich Meridian Line. It says so on my map, but there is nothing marking the spot. So not really sure. Let's say it is. That's more fun.

When you reach the next gate, you will be on a trail between fences and bush for a moment, then onto the road.

Now, if you want to go to the Abergavenny Arms, you can turn left. There is a trail sign for it. It's about 1/2 a mile down this road. From there, to get back to the trail, follow the main road towards Southease.

If not, go through this gate, and continue walking straight (in the same direction you got here). You will soon start to get a view of the farm buildings below. Now walk towards them. You should also start to see a road leading away from the farm, that's where you are heading to.

The first time I walked here, seeing the farm, I decided that maybe I will marry a farmer. Then I can live here. That was quite some years ago, and I haven't met any farmers yet. Where do farmers hang out?

Now when you reach the road, follow it. It's another long one. Longer than you will think. But the scenery is nice.

Walk to Southease

Before you reach the main road, there will be a trail on the right. Follow this, and it will lead you to the main road (at a better place than the other way).

At the road, walk straight across the triangle green, and continue along the road ahead to the left. This road will lead you down and to the River Ouse. You will pass by a church, and quite a few South Downs Way signs.

When you reach the river, if you want to get to the station, continue over the bridge, and it will be just ahead.

Walk back to Lewes

If you like beer, in Lewes there is an award winning brewery, the Beak Brewery. If you want to go there, then best walk on the trail on the other side of the river. That will lead you to it. If not, then stay on this side. There will be a gate on the left just before the bridge.

This bridge has a bit of history. It's called the Southease swing bridge. In the 18th and 19th centuries, this river was heavily used for transportation of goods to and from Lewes. The bridge would be swung open to allow passage through.

Through here you will have the option to walk along the riverside ridge, or below it to the left. The ridge is nicer, so I recommend that. But you can mix it up as you go along, as it's a long way. You can see Lewes from here, and it doesn't seem that far, but the river curves. It's about 4 miles to reach it, and you pretty much just follow the river until you get there.

There's nice views of the South Downs Hills, the chalk cliffs, meadows, and sometimes you will see the train going by.

As you get close to Lewes, the road noise really makes itself known. Stay following the path as it leads under the road bridge, and just keep to the river. There are a few other routes you can take at this point, but none of them escape the road, and I would say this is the most scenic way. There is a very big patch of mud you might have to navigate though. And it will try to suck your boot off.

After the mud patch, there will be a nice view across the other side of the river to the houses, and big white cliffs as you head into Lewes.

WALK 6

Southease to Seaford via Alfriston

To describe this walk, I would divide it into two halves, with a medieval village in the middle. The first half is along the hilltop, with all the views. The second half is more sheltered, with woods, marsh, and river, before finishing off with some cliffs. Some very famous cliffs actually.

The first time I did this walk, I actually didn't enjoy it. There were two reasons for this. One, it was blindingly sunny and very windy and I spent half the walk with the sun attacking my face and the wind trying to blow me away, and I could barely see with my eyes streaming with tears. Two, I needed a wee. For the first 5ish miles there is absolutely nowhere to hide, fully exposed on the hills.

I appreciated that it was probably a really good walk, so I gave it another chance in more favourable weather conditions, and made sure I had a wee before I set out.

From here you'll follow the river to reach the coast where you'll get a view along the gorgeous Seven Sisters Cliffs.

WHAT TO EXPECT

Out of the station, you'll reach the first hill pretty quick, then once up top, it's straightline walking pretty much most of the way to reach Alfriston, the 7 mile mark. It's a rather unique walk in that for a good chunk of this section, you can see your destination, walking parallel to the sea, on top of the hills of the South Downs.

Then you descend to reach Alfriston. A historic village surrounded by the beautiful countryside, with boutique and quirky shops, arts and antiques, a church and a pub from the 14th century.

The vibe of the walk changes after Alfriston, as you follow the river and walk through woods, with some hills and steps thrown in for good measure.

FUN FACT:
Cuckmere Haven, below the Seven Sisters Cliffs, was once a smuggling route. When the tide is out you can also see the remains of a shipwreck.

At the 10 mile mark, you'll then descend down to Exceat with the most incredible view along the Cuckmere River as it snakes through the valley. From here you'll follow the river to reach the coast where you'll get a view along the gorgeous Seven Sisters Cliffs. You now get to walk across cliffs (which means more hill) and along the seafront to reach Seaford.

DIRECTORY

LOGISTICS:

Start/Finish: Southease Station, Seaford Station. East Sussex.
Difficulty: Moderate/Challenging.
Type: Point to point.
Route Distance: 14.5 miles/23.5 km.
Time: 5–6h.

HOW TO GET THERE:

Southease and Seaford are on the same train line which makes things easy. From London Victoria, buy a return ticket to Seaford. You will have to change at Lewes, but from there, it's only one stop to Southease (this train then continues on to Seaford, so you can use your return to go home at the end).

COMING BY CAR:

Park in Seaford, at Richmond Road car park BN25 1DB or West Street car park BN25 1EE. From there, catch the train to Southease to start the walk.

ELEVATION GAIN:

543m/1782ft.

TERRAIN:

Grass, dirt, some mud if it's rained, stairs, promenade, road, 1 stile.

DOG FRIENDLY:

For the most part. The stile has a doggy door. However, there is some loose livestock about, and not much shelter for the first half of the walk. The main tricky part I would say is a wall to climb over. It's probably a couple of feet high.

PHONE SIGNAL:

Yes.

PUBLIC TOILETS:

Only towards the end of the walk. At the Seven Sisters Visitors Centre, and along the beach in Seaford. Unless you stop at one of the pubs along the route.

IDEAL TIME OF YEAR:

Anytime avoiding weather extremes, as it's very exposed for the first half of the walk.

OPTION TO SHORTEN THE WALK:

Yes. From Alfriston, you can catch bus 26 to Seaford. That would be a 7 mile walk. From Exceat you can catch the 12 coaster bus to Seaford. That would be a bit over 10 miles walk.

WHERE TO EAT?
CAFE AND COFFEE:

On the walk

- 7 miles: The Singing Kettle Teahouse, Alfriston (dog friendly terrace)
- 7 miles: Badgers Teahouse at The Old Village Bakery (weekday opening hours only), Alfriston (dog friendly).
- 10 miles: Saltmarsh Farmhouse and Cafe, Exceat (dog friendly).

PUB:

On the walk

- 7 miles: The George Inn, Alfriston (dog friendly).
- 8.5 miles: The Plough and Harrow, Litlington (dog friendly).

Seaford

- Steamworks Pub, Seaford (conveniently attached to the station/ dog friendly).

FOR SUPPLIES:

Village store in Alfriston.
Morrisons in Seaford.

TIPS/OTHER THINGS TO KNOW

- For the first 10 miles you will be following the South Downs Way. I have found it to be very well signposted, apart from the Alfriston area. So you can just follow those signs.

- If you'd like to make the walk longer, when you reach Exceat, stay following the South Downs Way across the Seven Sisters Cliffs, to reach Eastbourne where there is a train station. It's about 10 miles more from this point, and very very hilly. If you decide to do that, I salute you. It's tough.

- If it's a very sunny day, make sure you have sunglasses and a hat, as you will be facing the sun.

- The main mud will all be after Alfriston. Before that it shouldn't be too muddy.

- Hiking boots recommended.

If you catch it right, you may get to see ferries from France coming into port.

ROUTE DESCRIPTION

Often, to get to a walking trail involves a bit of navigation from the train station. Well, not on this one. The South Downs Way trail literally goes over the rail tracks. A nice easy way to start.

So, out of the station, turn right on the road.

Just before the big barn shed thing, there is a track to the right. There should be a South Downs Way sign on the wall. Follow it.

Then when you reach the big gate, turn left just before it. This will lead you over a bridge, and from there keep following the trail which will curve its way up the hill.

Walk to the top

Just past the next gate you will notice a trail offshoot up the hill to the left.

You can take either as they both lead to the same place. The top. The left trail is more direct, but it's steeper. The straight ahead trail is nice and gentle.

Taking the straight ahead trail, stay on it past a grass trail offshoot, and you will start to get sea views and the town of Newhaven to the right. If you catch it right, you may get to see ferries from France coming into port.

After the trail curves around, there will be multiple trail options. Take the left one, and then when you reach the fences with a trail through them and a trail on the left side, take the one on the left, so you end up walking with the fence to your right, with a view of the trees up ahead.

Further along, as the fence bends right, the trail will bend with it, still taking you uphill.

You are going to be walking in a rough straight line now for the next 6 miles or so to reach Alfriston. So through every gate, stay straight. There are a couple of very slight bends, which I will explain through the guide.

The highest point is about 3 miles from here. You won't be walking uphill the whole time. It's more of a gentle undulation. Sometimes level, sometimes up, sometimes down, with views of the villages down the hill to the left, and more hills and the sea to the right. You won't have a tonne of views ahead though. It's just a plain wall of green.

At some point you'll reach a mast. Something a little different to look at, to break up the plainness. After the mast, at a gate, you will be able to meet the farmer. There is a QR code for it.

Next you will reach Firle Beacon car park. Continue straight through it, then before the end, there is a gate to the left. It should be signposted with the South Downs Way. Walk through this, and continue straight again.

It's now a gentle uphill, with a couple more gates thrown in, to reach Firle Beacon which at 217m is the highest point in the walk. It's not the end of the hills though.

Walk to Alfriston

It's about 3 miles to reach Alfriston from here. From the trig point, bear right, so the fence is to your right, but you're not right up close to it. You will be walking downhill now, and instead of a view ahead of a wall of green, you will have the rolling hills with a view of the squiggly trail leading into the distance.

Continue on the squiggly trail, through a gate, and then another to reach the road and car park. Take the path that is on the right (but still walking in a straight direction from how you arrived, so the big car park is to your left).

It's a mini uphill now, then when you reach a V split, keep to the left, then at the fence corner, take the left, so the fence is on your right.

When you reach a gate on the right, go through it, then continue along the left side of a crop field. You'll have a view of Alfriston down in the valley from here.

Through the second gate, stay straight to now walk on a trail lined with trees. Continue all the way downhill, which will lead you to a residential area, where you stay straight. I told you it was a lot of straight.

Follow this road, which will bend a little, then when you reach the end, you will be in the village centre. The George Inn will be in front of you.

You can now have a little explore around the village.

Walk to Exceat

To continue on with the walk, you want to head to the church. Picking up from where we left off, with the George Inn in front of you, turn right, then take the first left along an alley. This will lead you to the church of St Andrew. It's about 3 miles to reach Exceat from here.

Standing facing the church, you want to take a path to the far left, which will be almost behind you. Follow this to find the white bridge, then cross over and turn right. You will now be following both the South Downs Way and Vanguard Way. This bit is along a grass ridge, surrounded by marsh, meadows, the Cuckmere River, and some cottage and church cuteness.

Through the third gate, follow the main gravel trail, then just before you reach the bridge, there is a trail to the left. Take it.

You'll now be on a very neat path through some trees to reach the road, where you turn right to walk past the Plough and Harrow. Following the road, when it curves to the right, you turn left. Then just before the private no entry sign, the trail is to the right, through a gate, and quite steeply uphill.

Follow this trail up the hill, and through the next gate stay straight to now walk along the right edge of a field. Soon you will get a view of some woodland ahead. That's Friston Forest. Where you are heading next.

Down the hill, at the end of the fields, there will be a stile to get you into the forest. When you enter, turn left.

Southease to Seaford via Alfriston

Quite soon you will reach the first steps. Go up them.

When you reach an open area, stay straight, and now stay on this main path ignoring all the trail offshoots. When you reach the end, turn right. This will lead you down to a road corner. Stay straight, past a cute house, to reach the next steps. These are the last ones.

At the top of these steps you will reach a stone wall, which you need to climb over. Now you will be rewarded with a stunning view down into the Cuckmere Valley, and the winding snakelike river running through it.

Over the wall, head straight down the hill to reach the road. You might see some horses here. At the road, you need to cross over it, and it's a tough one. I've had to wait up to 5 min for a gap in the cars to cross. It's harder on weekends – when there are more people out and about.

This is where you leave the South Downs Way (unless you have decided to stay on it and walk the Seven Sisters). There are also buses here if you'd like to end the walk.

Walk to Cuckmere Haven

Over the road, turn right. Now, the trail continues alongside the road for a bit. If you want to avoid the road, there is a way, but it's a big loop. To do the loop, walk through the car park to reach a trail, then follow it around the marsh and river bends. When you reach the main stretch of the Cuckmere River, turn right to walk with the river to your left, to get back to the road and bridge crossing. This will add about 1 mile to the walk.

I have no interest in adding an extra mile to what is already a long walk, so I choose to take the road. If you look to the left at the gorgeous views, you can pretend it isn't there. Once you reach the bridge, you will see the Cuckmere Inn on the other side.

To cross the bridge, you will need to go onto the other side of the road, then once over it, cross back over to walk into the car park. Through the other side of the car park is the trail. There will be a Chyncton Farm National Trust sign here.

Now follow this trail, first lined with bushes, then with views across the marsh and hills.

When you reach a junction, take the left, then a few meters along is a gate, you have two options here. Left will take you along the river to reach Cuckmere Haven. It's a lovely route, and doesn't add any extra distance. Do this if you want to go to the beach. I'm going to direct you through the gate though.

Following the trail through the gate, you will soon get a view to the Seven Sisters Cliffs, and after a couple more gates, the (probably most photographed) coastguard cottages up ahead. As you might have guessed, this is a good place to take a photo. To get that famous shot, continue a little up the hill until you have the cottages and cliffs in frame.

Walk to Seaford

From here, continue straight past the cottages so you are walking with the sea to your left. There will be some more great views and photos opportunities of the cliffs along here.

You are now going to follow the cliff coast all the way to Seaford. It's a bit hilly as you make your way over Seaford Head, and past a golf course.

Once you reach the top, you will have a wonderful view down over Seaford, and no more uphill. Yay.

Now make your way down to it, to reach the promenade. It's about 1/2 a mile along this promenade, alongside the shingle beach, passing a Martello Tower, and some beach huts along the way.

Keep an eye out for the big town centre sign which directs you to the right along West View road. Continue straight, joining onto Pelham Road, to reach the Morrisons. At Morrisons, turn right, then take the next left and you will reach the station.

WALK 7

Amberley to Arundel along the River Arun

This is a wonderful easy walk following the River Arun. But it's not just about the river. There's woodland, some hills, horses, a historic market town, and a castle.

The first time I did this walk, I wasn't expecting a lot. I tried it out because I wanted something simple and short. I was pleasantly surprised by what it offered, and have since been back many times in all seasons.

You could easily spend a good chunk of time here, so it's a good thing the walk isn't too long.

WHAT TO EXPECT

You get onto the river pretty soon out of the station, then just follow it, first through some fields, then all the woods. It can get pretty muddy through this bit. There's one section in particular which is quite aggressively muddy. So much so that there is a newly installed walkway to get you over it.

You then have a sneaky hill, but it's not too bad, and you'll leave the river briefly, passing by a farm and a very nice looking home. When you get back to the river, you need to cross over a stream on a plank of wood, which is very well hidden, and then you'll finish along a ridge next to the river, with a wonderful view to Arundel Castle. There is also a great pub here which you should stop in.

FUN FACT:

Arundel Cathedral was designed by the same guy who invented the first ever taxi. You know those horse drawn carriages from the olden days? That's called a Hansom Cab. His name is Joseph Hansom.

Then you reach Arundel. A historic market town, slightly on the posher side, with galleries, and independent vintage shops. A museum, cathedral and castle. Cafes, restaurants, pubs, and bars.

You could easily spend a good chunk of time here, so it's a good thing the walk isn't too long.

Amberley to Arundel along the River Arun

DIRECTORY

LOGISTICS:

Start/Finish: Amberley Station, Arundel Station. West Sussex.
Difficulty: Easy.
Type: Point to point.
Route Distance: 6 miles/9.5 km.
Time: 2h.

HOW TO GET THERE:

Both stations are on the Southern Railway route, one station apart. Buy a return ticket from London Victoria or Clapham Junction to Arundel, get off one stop early in Amberley to start the walk. Journey time 1h 20min.

COMING BY CAR:

Mill Road car park in Arundel (BN18 9PA). Pay parking. Then get the train to Amberley to start the walk.

ELEVATION GAIN:

195m/643ft.

TERRAIN:

Mud, dirt trail, grass, wooden walkway, some stiles.

DOG FRIENDLY:

Yes. There is one field with horses, another with sheep. Other than this, your dog can roam free. The stiles either have gaps big enough for a human to fit through, some have gate alternatives.

PHONE SIGNAL:

Yes.

PUBLIC TOILETS:

Yes. In Arundel Station.

IDEAL TIME OF YEAR:

All seasons are good, but just be aware it can get quite muddy after rain. Summer is quite pretty with all the flowers.

OPTION TO SHORTEN THE WALK:

Not if coming by train. By car, a nice option would be to park in Arundel, then follow the river to the Black Rabbit to eat, before following the river back. This will be about 3.5 miles total.

WHERE TO EAT?

You are spoilt for choice on this one. With options at the start, during, and end. In fact, Arundel has an unusual amount of top rated pubs, restaurants, and cafes. To keep this simple, I have listed places I have been to and recommend. But please feel free to research what else is about.

CAFE AND COFFEE:

Amberley

• Riverside Tea Rooms (dog friendly).

PUB:

On the walk

• 4 miles: The Black Rabbit (dog friendly).

FOR SUPPLIES:

Pallant of Arundel Deli in Arundel (they have nice cheese). Or Morrisons for less posh.

TIPS/OTHER THINGS TO KNOW

- I strongly suggest wearing waterproof hiking boots due to the mud. I've even encountered mud in summer.
- The walk can easily be done in either direction. I prefer this way though, as there is more stuff in Arundel. However, if you want to finish somewhere a bit more quiet and peaceful, then you might prefer walking it the other way.

> *Through one of the openings, make sure to look back to see the chalk cliff views.*

ROUTE DESCRIPTION

Out of the station, turn left to get to the main road, then left again and the river will be just ahead.

Cross over the bridge. There is no designated walking lane on the bridge so you need to be careful of the cars. Once across, go through the gate on the left to start the walk along the River Arun.

It's a little noisy along here with the road so near, but as you go further it will start to fade away.

The walk starts off along a grass ridge, to reach a field with horses. This is where it can start to get a little muddy.

The woods

Gradually things become more woody, with a section along a wooden plank type walkway. Although now engulfed in woods, there is the occasional opening to the left for a view along the river, and to the fields on the other side with the hills in the distance.

Through one of the openings, make sure to look back to see the chalk cliff views.

The uphill and the farm

After roughly 2 miles, the trail will take you away from the river and uphill to a gated field. There is a livestock sign here, although you are separated from the livestock by an electric fence. Follow the trail down the left edge of the field, and then back up another hill towards the farm.

The trail is just to the right of the farm building, and along it you will have a lovely view to some quaint buildings at the other end.

When you reach the driveway road, with a manor house ahead, turn right and walk past the 'rich person garage' to pick up the trail straight across on the other side. Maybe you will get to see another horse.

Walk back to the River Arun

Walk downhill along the trail and this will lead you back to the river. You might see some trains go by on the other side. At the bottom, keep following the trail, so the river is on your left.

Somewhere along here, just past one of the gates, look out for the plank of wood over the river branch. You need to cross this, so don't miss it. Sometimes it's hidden in overgrowth. Don't worry if you do miss it though, this trail will lead you to the road in Offham. When you get there, turn left then take the first right, and you will reach the Black Rabbit pub.

If you found the plank of wood to cross, turn right after to walk along a nice grassy path with the River Arun to your left. Occasionally you will see more trains pass by, and can say 'Choo Choo' as they run along. You will also start to get a view to Arundel Castle around here.

You will next reach the Black Rabbit pub. Being so close to Arundel, it's a great place to stop before finishing off the remainder of the walk along the river. It has a lovely riverside setting and views to Arundel Castle.

Walk to Arundel

Past the pub, there are a couple of options to reach Arundel, through nature reserve, or along the river. This guide will take you along the river, but feel free to do as you please.

So, past the pub, get back onto the trail on the left, and now follow this grassy ridge as it curves alongside the river, with more castle views to your right. This will lead you all the way into Arundel.

Amberley to Arundel along the River Arun

PUBLIC TRANSPORT

The Surrey Hills are extremely well connected to London with trains, and you can cover more of it by train journey than the other National Landscapes in the book (it helps that it is the smallest). All of the walks in this book you can get to in 30 min to just over an hour. These are the routes used:

London Victoria – Southern Railway.

London Waterloo – South Western Railway.

Clapham Junction – South Western Railway, Southern Railway.

WALK 8
Haslemere to Devil's Punch Bowl
7 miles

WALK 9
Guildford, St Martha's Hill, and Newlands Corner
11.5 miles

WALK 10
Leith Hill: Holmwood to Dorking
12 miles

WALK 11
Box Hill and the Stepping Stones
3.5 miles

WALK 12
Guildford to Godalming
6 miles

SURREY HILLS NATIONAL LANDSCAPE

In the Surrey Hills you will find a lot of woods, lots of hills with wonderful views, and it's where I go for a walk if I don't want to travel too far, as they are just south of London, with the South Downs connected below, and Kent Downs connected to the East.

Some of the most famous beauty spots, and well known hills are in here. From Box Hill, to Leith Hill, the North Downs Way 153 mile long distance trail. Although, that trail is a bit cursed for me. I've been attempting to complete it, but every time I go out for another section I seem to get injured.

Designated as an AONB (now National Landscape) in 1958, it was actually the second to be designated in the whole country. It covers 163 square miles, so is the smallest of the green spaces in the book. As it is a bit smaller, with lots of towns and villages in or surrounding it, you are never that far from civilisation. Which actually makes it a great place to walk if you don't want to be too remote.

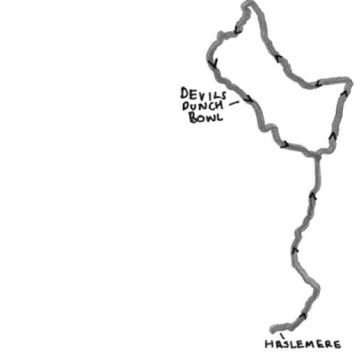

WALK 8

Haslemere to Devil's Punch Bowl

The star of the walk is Devil's Punch Bowl. This is something you need to come see for yourself. Pictures just don't do it justice.

It is essentially a deep crater in the earth, and has been described as a natural amphitheatre. The crater (bowl) is filled with all sorts of trees and an abundance of wildlife, and a place of Special Scientific Interest.

That's not the only good thing about the walk though. You will pass some historical points of interest (Temple of the Four Winds, the Celtic Cross), and be presented with insane far reaching views.

Once there, you can freestyle down in the crater.

WHAT TO EXPECT

There is a bit of road walking to reach the trail, and then it's pretty easy for a while, mostly through woods. Then it gets hilly. Very steep hilly, with some wonderful views to go with it.

After about 3.5 miles you will reach Gibbet Hill, the highest point in the walk, and then just a short way past here you will reach Devil's Punch Bowl. Once there, you can freestyle down in the crater. I will describe a route to you, but it's quite easy to get lost.

For this route, you will walk down into the crater and back up the other side, sometimes quite off-piste and rugged. At this point you will have walked about 5 miles.

FUN FACT:

Gibbet Hill is the second highest point in Surrey, with views to London on a clear day.

To get back to Haslemere it's about 3.5 miles, and involves some more woods, and some very steep hills, so if you've had enough, you can get the bus back from here.

DIRECTORY

LOGISTICS:

Start/Finish: Haslemere Station, Surrey.
Difficulty: Challenging.
Type: Circular.
Route Distance: 7 miles/11 km
Time: 3–4h.

HOW TO GET THERE:

Direct trains from London Waterloo and Clapham Junction, which takes approx 50m–1h.

COMING BY CAR:

National Trust car park at Devil's Punch Bowl (GU26 6AB) which is free for members or pay and display. Card payment accepted.

ELEVATION GAIN:

471m/ 1545ft.

TERRAIN:

Dirt trail, bridleway, mud, grassy trail, some road.

DOG FRIENDLY:

Yes, dogs are allowed at Devil's Punch Bowl but must be kept on a lead during bird nesting season (March–September).

PHONE SIGNAL:

Yes.

PUBLIC TOILETS:

Yes, at Haslemere Station and Devil's Punch Bowl.

IDEAL TIME OF YEAR:

August for the heather bloom.

OPTION TO SHORTEN THE WALK:

Yes. You can get the number 19 bus between Devil's Punch Bowl and the station. From Devil's Punch Bowl, if you walk out of the car park along London road, when you reach the big main road, the bus stop is on the opposite road past the roundabout.

WHERE TO EAT?

The only thing along the route is at Devil's Punch Bowl, but there are a number of options in Haslemere. Here are some suggestions:

CAFE AND COFFEE:

Haslemere

- The Courtyard Cafe (dog friendly).
- Hemingways of Haslemere (dogs outside only).

On the walk

- National Trust Cafe at Devil's Punch Bowl

PUB:

Haslemere

- The White Horse (dog friendly).
- The Swan Inn (dog friendly).

FOR SUPPLIES:

Waitrose in Haslemere.

TIPS/OTHER THINGS TO KNOW

- It can get very muddy, so I strongly recommend hiking boots.
- At Devil's Punch Bowl, there is an information board with more suggested routes you could try if you wish. I've described a route for you below, but feel free to do what suits you.
- There are some trails which are mountain bike routes, so be on alert in case any bikes suddenly appear.

*I'm not always a fan of
'civilised' on my walks,
but I rather enjoy this bit.*

ROUTE DESCRIPTION

Out of Haslemere Station, take a right to walk along the main road. Once through the bridge tunnel, take the first right to start the long walk uphill.

This road goes on longer than you think it will, passing by some nice homes. Probably rich people homes.

At the junction at the top, you will be greeted by a quirky hedge. Walk to the left of it. Now, you need to be a bit careful here, as there is no pavement, and there are cars.

Where the road splits, you can take either. I would recommend the right one though, leading to the retirement village. It's called Wispers Lane. I like that.

Slightly further along Wispers Lane, look out for a trail to the left which will take you alongside the road.

Walk through the strange but beautiful woodland

In the woods, soon you will feel like you are walking through grand, dense woodland. You'd forget you are walking right next to a road. If you look to your left and squint, you won't notice the houses on the other side of the woods, and will feel like you are deep in the forest.

Some of the trees here are massive, with branches and roots twisted about. Giving off a sort of fairytale vibe.

Walk onto the main path

You will reach a point where the trail splits at a tree. Remember this point. On the way back you will reach this point, then you can retrace your steps back to the station. There is a little green area here with a log that's good for sitting. Snack break log.

Right now, to make your way to Devil's Punch Bowl, take the left. It will take you onto the road path, which you continue straight on.

Next there is a bit of road to walk on. It's not a very busy one though. I think that only people who live along here drive this way.

This bit of the walk feels very civilised. It is also very deceptive for what the walk will be like later on. I'm not always a fan of 'civilised' on my walks, but I rather enjoy this bit, surrounded by all the trees, with the occasional opening to the right of the views.

When you reach the multi-trail signpost, continue straight.

Dream home

This trail leads you to a gate with a sign saying private property. Ignore that. It's a public right of way, so you can walk through. Whoever lives here has it made. The only downside is the walking trail running through, which takes away some of the privacy.

You are probably expecting some grand mansion or something. This is not that at all. First off, through the trees is a large green valley, with a lake and small lake house. Then further up, overlooking the valley is the main house. The view from the main house… wow. Living here, you would feel so secluded (except for the walking trail), in your own little valley.

Walk up to Hurt Hill (real name)

Past the house, you will continue straight on a dirt trail through more woodland.

At the junction, take the left fork. (Note, there is another left trail just next to the junction. I don't mean that one).

Now you go up.

This bit is very steep, and can be slippy if there is mud or leaves on the ground. It's actually a mountain bike track. As such, be careful and watch out for any mountain bikes that come shooting down.

At the top, take a look around for an insane view, reaching as far as the hills of the South Downs.

Walk to Temple of the Four Winds

Technically you aren't at the top yet, so after admiring the view, you need to continue up a little more.

Just past the viewpoint, you will reach another trail where you turn left(ish). There is a bit of a junction here. Once you have walked onto the trail, you will see a signpost. Don't follow the blue arrows. Instead, walk straight past it.

This will lead you to the Temple of the Four Winds.

Temple of the Four Winds

Not be confused with Temple of the Winds. When I first came here I was looking for a Temple. The Temple I saw pictures of online, and on Google Maps. There is no temple here. What we have here is a base. It turns out there is a Temple of the Winds which is a Temple up north. So Google has got them confused.

What my subsequent research told me is:
1. It was actually a lodge, with the name Temple of the Four Winds.
2. Built in 1910 by Viscount Pirrie.
3. Due to vandalism and falling into disrepair and becoming a hazard, it had to be dismantled in 1966.

I do have a laugh sometimes at the Temple mistake. The view from here is stunning though.

Walk to Gibbet Hill and Cross

So, the next big steep hill is coming up.

Continue on the trail past the 'Temple' (follow the yellow arrow). Along here, it's a mix of level trail and small uphill.

Stay on this main trail until you reach a big junction. There is a signpost here with lots of arrows. The trail you want is straight ahead. For reference, there is a little sign at the start of the uphill trail saying 'no cyclists'.

At the top of this trail, you will be at Gibbet Hill where there is a perfectly placed viewpoint bench. This is the second highest point in Surrey, and on a clear day, you can see as far as the London skyline (over 60km away).

Next, walk towards the Celtic Cross. This cross was erected by Sir William Erle (or rather, the people he paid to do it) as a way to banish the fears and superstitions surrounding Gibbet Hill. What happened is, in 1786 a sailor was brutally murdered here by three men whom he had befriended in a local pub. The three men were then hanged from Gibbet Hill as a warning to other criminals. There is a stone erected at the murder site, along Portsmouth Road.

Walk to Devil's Punch Bowl

Past the cross and through the gate, you will start to get a view across to Devil's Punch Bowl.

Walk down the trail to reach Portsmouth Road, then turn right. Walk along this road, and keep your eye out for a sort of hidden trail on the left, that will get you onto the trail around Devil's Punch Bowl. (If you want to see the Sailor's Stone, stay on this road. It's a little further along).

When I first started researching Devil's Punch Bowl, I just knew there would be some story about how it was created by the devil. We do love a good devil story. In this instance there are a few devil theories. I'm going to give you the gist of them:

- The Devil was irritated by all the churches being built in Sussex, so he decided to flood it all by digging a channel through the South Downs. During his mission, he got disturbed by a cock crowing and leapt into Surrey. Where he landed created this massive crater, now known to us as the Devil's Punch Bowl.
- To annoy the God Thor, he would scoop out bits of earth to throw at him. One of these scoops is the punch bowl. This is the story I like.

Walk down into Devil's Punch Bowl

Now walk to the right along the trail (the valley/crater on your left). Your view into the valley is sort of obscured a bit along here, by all the bush hedges.

At the junction, take the left trail and continue making your way downhill.

When you get to the road, walk through the gate on the left.

This next bit of the walk is my favourite bit. You will descend further down into the crater of Devil's Punch Bowl. It feels a bit like walking deep down into a hidden mysterious place, with the narrow winding trail, whilst being engulfed by all sorts of plants and woodland.

There is the occasional trail offshoot, but you mostly stick to the main trail. Keep an eye out for the orange arrows, and follow those.

Next the orange arrows will direct you onto an off-piste path, and you will feel like you are going the wrong way.

At times the trail is not obvious at all, and you need to just continue straight and trust that you are going in the correct direction.

Walk uphill out of Devil's Punch Bowl

Following the almost invisible trail, you will start to make your way uphill. When you reach the stump sign with the orange arrow partway up a hill, follow it to the left where you will be on a more obvious trail.

Now follow this to walk the rest of the way up.

Devil's Punch Bowl viewpoint

At the top you will have a lovely view across the crater, and to the hills in the distance. For an even better view, turn right at the top and walk towards the big open area.

If you have gotten lost (which might happen), don't worry, just look for the car park and National Trust Centre on Google Maps and this point is near there.

Walk through Hindhead Commons

Now, to continue the walk, it's the second left trail when you get to the top of the hill. Not the one with the gate.

So, if you are standing at the top of the uphill trail, take a right and immediate left.

To keep it simple, this next chunk of walk is in a straight(ish) direction. There are going to be various trail options, but stick to the one that keeps you going straight-ish.

You will be guided by the blue arrows now.

Keep going to reach an opening with a bench (the second one).

The next big descent

At this bench, there are two trails to the left of it. The bigger trail, and the smaller, more hidden trail. Take the smaller, more hidden trail.

The first time I was here was with my now ex-boyfriend, and once he realised what was happening, he immediately protested. I was taking him downhill. Steeply downhill. Which would mean a big uphill later. Plus the sun had set. It was dark.

The thing is, this is the most direct route to walk back to Haslemere. The alternative would be a big loop. After a bit of convincing he followed me down.

Just to prepare you, this bit is very steep and potentially slippy.

Walk through the valley

At the bottom you will reach a bigger trail and wooden signpost. Follow it to the right. Now, following this trail, it will lead you through a gate and across a road.

The trail will bend to the left at a 'private keep out' sign. Keep following it, under all the trees, with a fence to your right.

The last big uphill

You will reach a cross signpost. I liken it to a death cross, leading you to the death hill.

Continue straight past it to make your way steeply uphill for the last time. At the top, the trail isn't too obvious. Basically, you need to continue a bit straight and to the left, where you will find the main trail.

At this main trail, turn right.

Walk back to Haslemere

You will now walk downhill along this road trail carved out between the trees.
A bit further along, follow the road trail as it curves to the right. Soon the trail will turn from dirt to road as you approach some houses.

You will start to see through the trees to the left, a very ornate looking house.

There is a sort of a haunted house vibe to it.

When you reach the junction with the haunted looking house, walk up the road on the left, so the house is on your right. Ok, I lied. There is a bit of uphill here. But it's nothing compared to the other hills so I don't consider it a hill today.

This road will soon lead you to the point I told you about earlier on to remember for the walk back to Haslemere, with the open green area and snack log. You can now walk back the way you came. There is another way back, but I don't like it. Although, to be fair, I did that route in pitch black. It was a bit scary through the straggly woods.

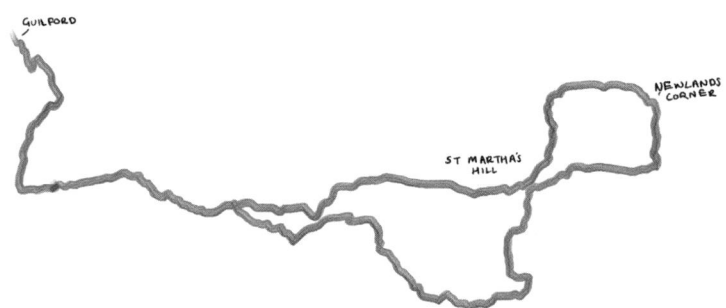

WALK 9

Guildford, St Martha's Hill, and Newlands Corner

This is a solid walk across the Surrey Hills and North Downs Way, with a bit of everything. A gentle river, woodland with trees so big they engulf you, open fields and hills with views, a bit of war history, and a Grade II listed hilltop church. 175m high to be exact.

I love the variety of this walk, and although I have never been a history buff, I really enjoy seeing the gunpowder mills.

The hard work is pretty much done now. The remaining hills are gentle(ish).

WHAT TO EXPECT

There is a bit of road navigating to start, to reach the River Wey. From there you follow the river for a short while, which is quite lovely, before heading across a sports field and along a bit more road to reach Chantry Wood.

There is a chunky uphill now, before things level out, and there's a surprise view to the Guildford Cathedral perfectly framed through the trees. You won't know it's there unless you know where to look, which I explain in the route description.

Chantry Wood is pretty huge, 200 acres huge in fact, but for now the route will only take you through a small part of it (you will return for more later). Out of the woods there is a bit of hilltop view goodness, before you descend, which is quite rugged in parts, and then head over to the Chilworth Gunpowder Mills.

There used to be free information leaflets, but it's now been modernised and there are QR codes throughout, telling you all the info about what you are seeing.

FUN FACT:

In 1926, Agatha Christie staged her disappearance from Newlands Corner. She was found later in Harrogate.

Out the other end, you'll then head back uphill and then along the Pilgrims' Way with a really cool view up to Newlands Corner. You'll have this view for a while, giving you lots of time to think about how you need to walk up it next. Although, it's one of those hills which isn't as bad as it looks.

Once up the top of Newlands Corner you'll walk across the top of the grass slope, with those wonderful views, as you turn to make your way back to Guildford. There is of course another downhill and uphill first, to take you to St Martha's Hill. The hard work is pretty much done now. The remaining hills are gentle(ish) as you make your way back to Guildford through Chantry Wood, engulfed by those massive trees.

DIRECTORY

LOGISTICS:

Start/Finish: Guildford Station, Surrey.
Difficulty: Moderate.
Type: Circular.
Route Distance: 11.5 miles/18.5 km.
Time: 4–5h.

HOW TO GET THERE:

Direct trains from London Waterloo and Clapham Junction. There are fast and slow trains, so journey time varies between 30min and 1h.

COMING BY CAR:

Farnham Road car park by the station, GU2 7NP. Pay and display. For free parking (at the time of writing) you have Chantries car park GU4 8AW, near the woods, so you would skip the first bit out of Guildford, it's 5h max stay. Or Halfpenny Lane car park GU4 8PZ, and Guildford Lane Car park, GU5 9BQ. These are at St Martha's Hill, so you would be starting the walk from there.

ELEVATION GAIN:

623m/2060ft.

TERRAIN:

Dirt path, grass, bridleway, road, muddy after rain. No stiles.

DOG FRIENDLY:

Yes. Never seen loose livestock. However, there are a few roads to be cautious of.

PHONE SIGNAL:

Yes.

PUBLIC TOILETS:

Yes, at Guildford Station.

IDEAL TIME OF YEAR:

Spring for the bluebells, or autumn for the colourful leaves. If you are up for a bit of a dip in the river, then summer would be good for that.

OPTION TO SHORTEN THE WALK:

Not without missing out on something, but here are some options if you don't mind that. Guildford to St Martha's Hill – 7 miles out and back. Guildford to St Martha's Hill and Newlands Corner – 9 miles out and back. Guildford to the Chilworth Gunpowder Mills and St Martha's Hill – 8.5 miles circular. I have detailed how to do each one in the route description.

WHERE TO EAT?

Nothing along the route. Guildford at the start is a big town with lots of options. Here are a few suggestions.

CAFE AND COFFEE:

Guildford

- Frida's Coffee House (by the river/ dog friendly).
- The Boathouse Cafe (by the river/ dogs allowed outside).

PUB:

Guildford

- The White House (by the river/ dog friendly).
- The Kings Head (dog friendly).

FOR SUPPLIES:

Multiple supermarkets around town. For convenience there is an M&S at the station.

TIPS/OTHER THINGS TO KNOW

- Definitely wear hiking boots.
- During summer, the river section will be very busy. The banks lined with people doing river stuff. So I now avoid this area in summer.
- There is a bit of a lost-in-the-woods vibe for some of it, I personally never feel unsafe, but if you get nervous with that sort of thing, then best to do this walk with a friend.
- During popular times, the river, St Martha's Hill and Newlands Corner will be a bit busier, but the rest of the route not too much.

> *This whole area is actually a popular wild swim dipping spot.*

ROUTE DESCRIPTION

When you arrive in Guildford, you need to make your way to the River Wey. It's a little confusing out of the station. First exit the station at the town centre exit, then go under the underpass on the right past the bike racks.

On the other side, walk to the river, then turn right. Keep going to reach the bridge and White House pub. If you time it right, there will be penis shaped shadows on the bridge.

Walk along the river on the pub side to reach the next bridge. Cross over it, and then the other bridge straight after. This will lead you back to the main road, at which you turn right. From here, keep going past the car park and pub to reach the green field. It's about 5 min of walking along this road.

Walk along the River Wey

There are three trails in the field, take the one which runs along the river.

The next bit is easy. Simply walk along the River Wey (with the river to your right), under some trees, with views to houses on the other side, under some more trees, until you reach the bridge.

In the warm (when they happen) summer months, kids like to jump off this bridge into the river (although, I don't think thats allowed). This whole area is actually a popular wild swim dipping spot.

Walk to Chantry Wood

Just before the bridge, there is a trail to the left. Walk along it, past more trees and into an open field. Walk to the other side of the field, and you should see a wooden signpost for Chantry Wood. Follow it directly across onto a residential street.

Keep going, and a bit further along, you will reach a road forking to the right with another Chantry Wood sign. Take it.

You will start to walk uphill, past a car park, to a quaint white cottage. Walk to the right of the cottage, through the long metal gate, and continue straight and up into Chantry Wood. It's quite steep here, with a mix of dirt trail and steps.

Keep going up, and when you reach the junction, turn right to continue uphill some more.

Top tip: As the trail levels out, look out for a green on the left. Go and stand at the bench, and look straight ahead. You will get a fantastic tree framed view of the Guildford Cathedral.

At the second right trail past the viewpoint, turn onto it. Keep going, and after it curves around to the left, look out for a trail on the right which will lead you to a gate out of the woods.

Option to shorten the walk: Guildford to St Martha's Hill – 7 miles out and back. To do this, don't turn right after the cathedral viewpoint, stay straight. At the next junction, take the right, which then curves left. Now follow this straight all the way to reach the road. From there you can follow the North Downs Way signs to reach St Martha's Hill.

Guildford to St Martha's Hill and Newlands Corner – 9 miles out and back. Follow the above directions, then after St Martha's Hill, continue following the North Downs Way, and you will reach Newlands Corner.

The first viewpoints

Sticking with the main route, Once through the gate, turn left to walk along the trail. You will have some great views along here, but there are more to come, with benches, so hang on.

A bit further along, you will see a trail to the right through a gate. You can take that one or stay on this one, they join up in a minute.

Once past some bushes, and into the next field, walk to the right to take you along the edge of it. Here you will reach the High Ball viewpoint, with some benches to sit to enjoy the fantastic view.

Walk down off the hill

From the viewpoint, you will see the trail continues along the edge of the hill. Follow it.

Where it splits, keep to the right trail so you stay on the edge. You will walk through a metal gate, and a bit further along, you will see a gate to the left. Don't take that gate. Stay on the trail to the right. It's not obvious, and you might think you are going the wrong way. But trust me. There are actually two right trails, take the farthest right which goes steeply downhill.

Just a warning, this next bit is very off-piste and could have some overgrowth.

As you make your way down, start to bear left, and you should reach a trail at the bottom, to take you into some woods. Continue down through the woods, and possible overgrowth, then at the bottom, turn right after the very big tree.

Here you will see a hedge with a trail on the left and field on the right. Walk in the field, keeping to the left side.

When you reach the other end of the field, go through the gate on the left to reach the road. You might be horrified for a moment here. I certainly was the first time. You are on a very narrow country road bend, but don't panic! You don't have to walk on this road. Hidden just to the right, maybe 2 meters along the road, is a trail.

Walk to the Chilworth Gunpowder Mills

You will now walk between hedge and fence, then hedge and field. Along here is a view to the left of St Martha's Church up on the hill. Depending on the time of year and how bushy the trees are, you might have to look really hard to spot it just poking through.

At the end of this trail, you will reach another road corner with a nice house. Walk to the right and over a bridge.

Not too much further along, to the left, you will see a big green gate and wooden sign pointing to the Gunpowder Mills. Now just walk through. There is one trail you follow through here, and QR codes next to each item/building you see.

It's over 300 years old, and during the first half of the 17th century, was the sole producer of legal gunpowder in England to the King. It ceased production at the end of World War 1.

Here are a few bits of interesting information:
- In the early 1900's, there were 300 male workers and six female.
- Each morning they would be checked for items that could cause a spark, and would hang their smoking pipes in a nearby tree, to then collect at the end of the day.
- They would wear brimless hats, designed to keep gunpowder out of their hair. This avoided accidents at home when they sat by the fire.
- Once in barrels, the gunpowder would be sent to London along the Wey Navigation (the river you walked along earlier).

The first thing you will see as you enter the Chilworth Gunpowder Mills, is a white building on the right. This is a gate house, and is where workers were checked for any items that might cause a spark. At various points you'll see little cone shaped things on the ground. These are Dragon's Teeth, which marked defence lines, also known as GHQ stop lines. They prevented tanks from getting through. You'll also pass these big circular things. These are some millstones, and were placed on their sides to provide protection from accidental blasts. Each one weighs about three tonnes..

The trail will then take you past a green with some picnic benches, and then a tree lined trail. At the end of the tree lined trail, take a left, and to your right will be the ruins of a boiler house.

Walk to Newlands Corner

As you exit the Gunpowder Mills, you will reach a road. Turn left, and continue past the Longfrey Farm sign, then at the next junction go right. This will lead you onto a narrow dirt trail which guides you slowly uphill.

Where the trail splits, with steps to the left, you keep right. You will get some nice views down the hill from up here, before plunging into tree tunnel.

Past the most dense bit of tree tunnel, look out for a log up the bank to the right, with a gorgeous view down. There is a nice 'sitting' log here, if you want a break. Past the log, Keep going up, then when the ground levels off, you should see a war pillbox. These were used as defence lines in the war, with little holes to fire weapons out of.

Option to shorten the walk: You have the option to miss out Newlands Corner and walk straight to St Martha's Hill. At this point, turn left, following the North Downs Way signs, and you will reach St Martha's Hill. You can then continue my route description from that point (see St Martha's Hill).

To continue on to Newlands Corner, walk to the right of the pillbox, following the big trail through the woods.

When you reach a multidirectional, potentially confusing junction, walk to the bigger trail signpost on the right, and follow the left arrow. This will lead you to the road.

If you took the wrong junction, you should still end up on the road, but just at the wrong point. You should see a trail directly across the other side of the road. If you don't see it, then follow the road to reach it. It's just to the right of the car park for reference.

This next trail is the Pilgrims' Way. A long distance walking trail. The first time I did this walk, I got deja vu at this point. I'd driven past here before, and the views made me do a double take. I knew I had to come back and walk here someday, but then forgot about it. I hadn't realised I would be walking it on this day.

There is a fantastic view to the left here, up a big hill. That's Newlands Corner. The next stop. Continue following this trail, and after a bit of downhill, you'll reach a junction. Go left here, to walk past the farm buildings.

At the end, past the farm house, there is a nice looking trail to take you straight up that hill.

At the top of the hill, go through the gate (but look back at the view first), then walk up some more. Basically keep going up until you can't go up anymore, then turn left. This is where the magic happens. A sweeping view of the undulating hillside green, with far reaching views to the left.

Newlands Corner is actually spread across 250 acres of chalk grassland and woodland. But for this walk you just walk along the edge. It's also a popular spot for astronomers. Being close to London, but with a south facing slope to the dark sky, numerous constellations can be visible.

You now want to walk to the other end. There are a few benches dotted along the top, if you fancy a little break to admire the views.

Ahead to the left you will see a big hill with trees. That's the next hill. St Martha's Hill. Unfortunately, you will need to walk all the way down, to then walk up it. You're welcome.

Walk to St Martha's Hill

When you reach the end at the bushes, look out for a trail to the left. There should be a North Downs Way signpost here, but on my most recent visit, it was missing. You are going to be following the North Downs Way for some time now, which is well signposted (apart from this spot).

This left trail will take you under the trees, and downhill to reach the road. Directly opposite the road are some steps, go up them. Now follow the trail to the left. It runs alongside a road, but you are separated from it by a hedge, so you can pretend it's not there. Keep going down along the trail, and when the hedge disappears it will feel like the trail has ended. It hasn't. Keep going in the same direction, and you will be led under quite an interesting tree tunnel.

At the end with the house, follow the North Downs Way signposts which guide you around the left side of it.

Now it's the last uphill of the walk. Actually, I lie. It's the last big uphill of the walk. There are some smaller ones later.

Walk uphill through the woods, in the general direction of straight, then at the main (and sandy) path, turn right. If in doubt, follow the North Downs Way signs.

Continue uphill some more, and you will eventually reach the top of St Martha's Hill, with the church ahead of you.

The original church here was from the 12th century, but it fell into ruin by the 18th century and was rebuilt in the 19th century, ensuring that the original architectural features were included.

There are some wonderful views from up here. There's the obvious one, but if you go into the wooded area behind the church, you will see a lovely view to a Manor House between the tree trunks.

Walk back through Chantry Wood

To leave St Martha's Hill, on the other side of the Church (from the direction you arrived), take the bigger obvious trail.

You are still following the North Downs Way signage. If my directions confuse you, then just keep following it, and I will tell you when to stop following it.

Continue on through the woods, then when you reach a green where the trail spilts, take the left one. At the road, cross straight over it to continue along the trail on the other side. It will lead you back down to the road, where you turn left. Be careful here, as it's a narrow country road without much in the way of pavements.

You don't have to go too far though. Just ahead, at the road bend, walk into the woods on the right. There is an open area here, with a few trails. The right trail is the North Downs Way. Don't take it. Instead, take the trail that leads past the information board into the grand woodland.

Grand is an understatement. It's quite something in here. I think this is the most impressive woods I've seen near London. It feels a bit like it will swallow you whole.

For this next bit, the walk will be in a general straight direction, with some small curves, and hills. There is a point where the trail plunges down into a dip in the hill, then back up.

The first time I walked through here, it was dark. My ex-boyfriend and I had walked to St Martha's Church for sunset. When we arrived at this dip in the woods, all we could see was a black hole. It was very spooky. If I was on my own, I probably would have cried.

When you reach the dip, go down it, then back up the other side, keeping straight(ish). When you reach a junction on the edge of the woods, turn left, and you will be back on the main trail from earlier on in the walk. The one with the cathedral viewpoint.

Walk back to Guildford

From here, you can make your way back to Guildford the way you came. If you aren't sure (because sometimes walking back on yourself can be confusing), I will explain…

Stay on this trail, then when you reach the bench, take the left trail which will lead you out of the woods back to the white walled cottage. Follow the road, then turn left onto the residential street. At the other end, cross the road and green, and you will reach the River Wey.

From here, it might be nice to finish on the other side of the river. See things from a different perspective.

So, cross over the bridge, and turn right. Make sure though, to cross the black metal bridge when you reach it. If you stay along the river you will reach a dead end.

Over the bridge, turn left and you will be back in town.

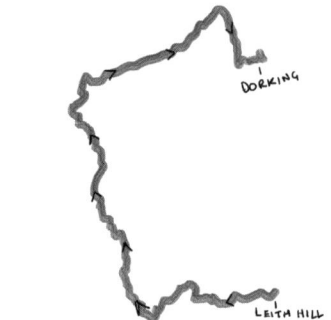

WALK 10

Leith Hill: Holmwood to Dorking

Leith Hill is a classic place to come for walks near London, where on a clear day you can actually see London. I also read that you can see up to 13 counties. 13 seems a bit far-fetched, but that's what they say. It is very impressive up there though.

There are a number of ways you can walk to it, but I've chosen to show you the quickest way up there, it's just under 3 miles from the station. This isn't a short walk though. Leith Hill is just the start. You'll then be immersed in miles of woods, walk along the North Downs Way with vast views across the vale, and finish off at a vineyard.

You can just walk straight through, or stop off for some wine.

WHAT TO EXPECT

The first part of the walk from the station is quite a bit of road, with some woods and fields thrown in, to reach Coldharbour with the pub and village store. From there it's a short uphill to reach Leith Hill. This is the 3 mile mark. From there you'll head deep into the woods. There are a lot of trails about to confuse you, hopefully my route description will keep you on track, but make sure you have a map as well.

It's roughly 3 miles through here, and you'll pass Friday Street with the pond and quaint cottages. At the 7 mile mark you'll reach Wotton, with a pub, and from there it's a short uphill, past a church, where you'll get a great view to a big hill and ridge ahead. That's the North Downs Way. You'll then head up there and follow the North Downs Way for almost the rest of the way to Dorking, with wonderful views down into the vale.

FUN FACT:

At 294m, Leith Hill is the second highest hill in South East England. The fun part is that the tower on Leith Hill was built so that when you stand on the top of it, at 313m you are now on the highest point in South East England.

There is a 78 step spiral staircase to get you to the top.

Towards the end, you'll turn in to walk through Denbies Wine Estate. You can just walk straight through, or stop off for some wine stuff. Then it's a short bit of road to reach the station. Just a note, the station isn't in the main part of Dorking town with all the shops. It's a good 10min walk further if you'd like to stop off there.

Leith Hill: Holmwood to Dorking

DIRECTORY

LOGISTICS:

Start/Finish: Holmwood Station, Dorking Station. Surrey.
Difficulty: Moderate/Challenging.
Type: Point to point.
Route Distance: 12 miles/19 km.
Time: 4–5h.

HOW TO GET THERE:

Direct trains from London Victoria on Southern Railway. Buy a return ticket to Holmwood, which will cover your return from Dorking. Journey time is just over 1h.

COMING BY CAR:

There are a few car parks around the Leith Hill and woods area. You'd modify the route a bit though. In fact, I'd just freestyle at this point. You can park in Coldharbour, just up the road from the pub. The parking isn't marked on maps. It's the uphill road off the main road by the pub, pub postcode is RH5 6HD. Other nearby options are Broadmoor car park RH5 6JY, or Shoe Tree car park RH5 6LX. (All are free at the time of writing).

ELEVATION GAIN:

666m/2185ft.

TERRAIN:

Grass, dirt trail, mud, a bit of road, stiles.

DOG FRIENDLY:

Yes. Any stiles have doggy holes.

PHONE SIGNAL:

Patchy. There are big stretches in the woods without signal.

PUBLIC TOILETS:

In Dorking Station only, unless you stop in one of the pubs or the vineyard.

IDEAL TIME OF YEAR:

Autumn for the colourful leaves, summer for the grapes.

OPTION TO SHORTEN THE WALK:

Only if you miss out on something, or come by car. If you just want to see Leith Hill, then once you get there, you can turn back the way you came. That would be 6 miles. You can also start from the next station down, Oakley, and do a loop.

WHERE TO EAT?
CAFE AND COFFEE:

On the walk

- Just under 3 miles: A kiosk style place serving drinks and snacks at Leith Hill (seasonal).
- Denbies Wine Estate, Dorking (restaurant and takeaway cafe/ dog friendly).

PUB:

On the walk

- 2 miles: The Plough Inn, Coldharbour (dog friendly).
- 6 miles: The Wotton Hatch (dog friendly).

FOR SUPPLIES:

Convenience store at Coldharbour.

TIPS/OTHER THINGS TO KNOW

- Leith Hill is very popular, so it might be a bit congested up there on weekends. I personally avoid it in the summer months for this reason. The rest of the woods is much quieter though.
- The tower is seasonal. It's closed over winter, and when it is open, it's just on weekends. To go up it, it costs £3, but is free for National Trust Members.
- Hiking boots definitely.
- There are no trains to Holmwood on Sundays.
- If coming by car, Coldharbour is a small area so spaces are limited.

You are now going deep into the woods, and will feel like you are in some far away land.

ROUTE DESCRIPTION

Out of the station, turn left, then a short way along look out for the trail on the left. There will be a big metal gate, with the trail to the right of it.

You will be on a narrow trail between bushes. This will lead you onto a road, where you continue straight along it.

It's a bit of a walk along this road now, it's not too bad, and has a verge you can walk on for some of it. After about 1/2 a mile, you will reach a junction with a trail sign. You want to stay on the road up the hill, which will then lead onto a dirt trail and into the woods.

Keep straight through these woods, to reach the road where you turn right.

Follow the road, passing an impressive house, then after about 150m there will be a field to the left. Go over the stile into it, and continue straight across the field.

When you reach the end, turn right onto the trail, and when you reach an opening with a stile on the left and road to the right, take the right.

A short way up the road, there is a trail on the right, into the woods. Take it.

It's quite wild here, but there is one trail through, so you shouldn't get lost.

Keep following it and it will lead you to a stile into a field. Continue across the field, keeping to the right, and on the other side there will be a stile onto a very narrow trail where you will be squished by hedges. It's only a short way, and you will reach the road with the Plough Inn pub to the right.

Nearly there.

There will be a green and car park on your left, walk around it, and start to make your way up the hill.

At the next car parking area, go through it to the trail on the left, and now stay on this main obvious trail. Just after it curves to the left, it's one final short uphill to reach the Leith Hill Tower.

You can now enjoy all those views.

Walk into the woods

If you stand on the left side of the tower, with the south view behind you, you want to take the trail that's diagonal left, at about 10 o'clock. Now head into the woods, then when you reach the first junction, take the right, and then stay on this main trail in a rough straight direction, ignoring any offshoot trails. I will tell you where to go at the bigger trail junctions.

You are now going deep into the woods, and will feel like you are in some far away land. If it was crowded at Leith Hill, it won't be through here.

When you reach a fork, take the right.

Then when you reach the U-bend in a dirt track, take the right, then a short way along look out for a little trail leading off it to the left.

After about 100m or so (not sure how good my judgement is), look out for a hidden almost missable trail to the left. This bit is very rugged and off-piste, but not for too long, as it leads you to a road. Look out for a random chimney as you make your way up.

At the road, turn right, then when you reach a car park, you will see a wide opening with a trail to the left. Take it. This leads you into Severells Cops. It's now a nice wide grass trail for a bit.

When you reach the end, turn right.

Friday Street

Follow this to the end, then turn left. This will lead you to the Mill Pond and Friday Street area. It's quite lovely here, and I wonder who lives in these little cottages. I'm a bit jealous.

If you want some eggs, you can pick them up from here. Just leave the cash and take the eggs.

Now walk to the left on the road, alongside the pond, then turn right to walk past the cottage. There is a big sign which says private property. Ignore that. You can walk there.

Walk to Wotton

You are kind of in Wotton already, but now you head to the main road, pub, and village hall. At the end of this next road, you'll reach another cottage and a road sign saying 'High Trees' in front of some very high trees. Turn left here.

You'll be on a nice wide path, then through a gate, and surrounded by some trees with a field below to the left.

When you reach an open area, take the trail on the right, up the hill, and stay on this trail which will lead you to a stile and out of the woods.

You'll now be on a trail lined with fence, through the middle of a field, downhill then up again. When you reach the road, don't go onto it, but instead, go into the field. You need to stick to the trail here. You are warned of that as you enter.

Walk to the other end of this field and out the other side, passing the Wotton Village Hall. At the main road, just to the left is The Wotton Hatch Pub.

Walk to the North Downs Way

At the road, cross over to the other side and along the road directly opposite, with a sign pointing to the Church of St John the Evangelist.

Follow the road and up the hill to reach the church.

As you make your way there you will be able to see a hill ahead. That's where you are heading next.

Take the trail to the left of the church, which unfortunately takes you downhill. It will lead you to a field with an obvious trail running across it. Follow that, towards an enviable home ahead with barn sheds.

When you reach the road, continue straight across on the track that leads to that hill.

Through the gate you will be in White Down Lease. You are going to do a C here. So take the trail to the left which then curves back around, like a C. Then once you've completed the C, you will reach a trail split. Take the left which leads you up that hill. It's a juicy hill, but my gosh the views are incredible.

At the top (well, near the top) you will reach a pillbox, and a gate. Welcome to the North Downs Way. You can now follow the North Downs Way signs for the next 2ish miles. I

know that signs sometimes like to go missing, so I will explain the route anyway.

Through the gate, continue up some more, then take the right at the junction.

You are going to stay walking in this direction, on this main trail with the hill drop down to the right, for the next mile and a half or so. There aren't a lot of views at first, the trees are in the way. But as you get further along, it all opens up, and you get a spectacular view across the Surrey Hills, and then down to Dorking.

When you reach Steers Field, there will be two trails ahead of you. Take the right one, then before you reach the other side of the field, go to the left where you will see a signpost for the North Downs Way. Follow this, then through a gate to reach the road.

Cross over the road to go on the road straight across. This will lead you past the St Barnabas Church. Continue along the green past the church, and after a few hundred meters look out for a trail on the left. It's the one with a trail sign.

Walk to Denbies

You'll now walk through some woods, and tight bush spaces, staying in the same direction, and across a road.

When you reach a proper junction, turn left, then stay straight at any trail offshoots. You will now start to descend the hill, and reach a trail with a large field to the left, and the woods to your right.

When you reach the bottom, turn right on the road, and follow this as it then leads onto the trail again. When you reach the end, you should see a gate leading out of the woods ahead. Go through there.

This will lead you into the Denbies Vineyard.

Now stay straight along the edge, passing the rows of grapes, and you will reach the big main path which you can take to the main building, if you want to do some wine stuff.

Walk to Dorking Station

For the station, stay on this trail up here (or come back to it if you went and had some wine), and follow it right to the other end, where you will reach a gate.

Go through the gate, and uphill a little and you will reach a residential area road. On the road, take the first left, past the houses, then the first right, then a left on the main road. Follow this to the end, and Dorking Station will be on the other side to the right.

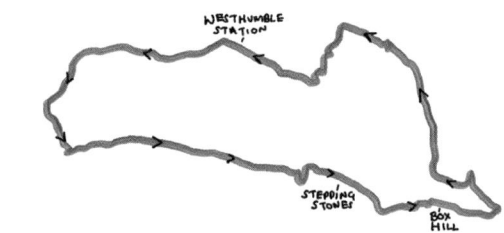

WALK 11

Box Hill and the Stepping Stones

This is a pretty famous walk in the south east of England. Located in the Surrey Hills, with infamous steps, incredible views, a road used in the Olympics, and stepping stones. Who doesn't love stepping stones?

The highest point is 224m, however, the famous viewpoint is lower down at 172m, at the Salomons Memorial. The area is owned by National Trust, who it was donated to by Leopold Salomons. He bought it 1914 to protect it from development.

I like to come and do this walk if I want something that isn't too long, but will give me a good workout… I always have a bit of regret though, when I'm making my way up those steps.

You then finish off along the stepping stones, before returning to the station (or the pub).

WHAT TO EXPECT

Steps. Steps of doom. The steps are pretty early on in the walk, to get you up Box Hill. No warming up for this one. Just before that though, you will cross over the River Mole over the memorial bridge which was erected in 1992 to replace the original bridge. It was presented by the Ramblers Association in memory of its members that died in WWII.

Once you make it up the steps, you will be rewarded with a fantastic view down to Dorking and across the Surrey Hills. You will then walk through woodland with box trees, which is where Box Hill gets its name (the trees don't look like boxes).

FUN FACT:

That Olympic road I mentioned is called Zig Zag. It was resurfaced for the 2012 Olympic cycling and is perfectly smooth.

You then leave the woods for a steep down then uphill, crossing over the Olympic road before circling back, passing by a very interesting grave (more on that later), and then back to those steps. Down this time.

You then finish off along the stepping stones, before returning to the station (or the pub).

DIRECTORY

LOGISTICS:

Start/Finish: Box Hill and Westhumble Station, Surrey.
Difficulty: Moderate. The hills are a little challenging but the rest is easy.
Type: Circular.
Route Distance: 3.5 miles/5.5 km.
Time: 1.5–2h.

HOW TO GET THERE:

Direct trains from London Victoria, London Waterloo, and Clapham Junction. Journey time between 35–50 min depending on the train.

COMING BY CAR:

The Stepping Stones National Trust car park RH5 6AE at the start of the trail (if starting from here, the left trail will take you to the memorial bridge, the right trail will take you to the stepping stones). The Box Hill National Trust car park KT20 7LB, at the top of Box Hill if you want to avoid the torture. It's free for members or Pay by Phone app.

ELEVATION GAIN:

295m/968ft.

TERRAIN:

Dirt, mud, steps, grass, steps, steps, some road, lots of steps. One stile.

DOG FRIENDLY:

Yes. The stile has a doggy hole. Never seen loose livestock.

PHONE SIGNAL:

Yes.

PUBLIC TOILETS:

Yes, at the National Trust car park on Box Hill.

IDEAL TIME OF YEAR:

Autumn is the perfect time, with all the autumn leaf goodness. I'd avoid the height of summer as it's extremely popular and will be very crowded.

OPTION TO SHORTEN THE WALK:

Yes. You can just walk up to the Box Hill viewpoint and hang around there before heading back down. It's a nice spot to take a picnic and sit admiring the views. Out and back will be about 2 miles.

WHERE TO EAT?
CAFE AND COFFEE:

Box Hill

- National Trust Cafe (although it's slightly off this route).

PUB:

Near the station

- Stepping Stones Pub (dog friendly).

FOR SUPPLIES:

None.

TIPS/OTHER THINGS TO KNOW

- I recommend hiking boots. This will help with grip on the hills. If it's been raining, there will be mud and big puddles.
- Be aware that if there has been recent heavy rain, the river level will be high, and the stepping stones will disappear. So take the bridge instead.
- There are a few benches at the top (but not many).

*Then when you think
you are about to suffer death by steps, there are
some more.*

ROUTE DESCRIPTION

Out of the station, head to the main road and turn right. Walk down it and past the Stepping Stones pub to reach the big road. Don't worry, you don't need to cross it. You can walk under it. The under road subway is to the left.

Once on the other side of the road, you will see a North Downs Way sign pointing right. Ignore that, and turn left, and the trail will be on your right.

Stay straight through the field, with the big hill ahead of you. That's THE hill.

You will then reach the stepping stones memorial bridge.

Cross over the bridge, and continue following the main trail straight. You will pass the junction which leads back to the stepping stones (this is where you go for the walk back). Don't go that way yet.

The steps and Box Hill

After a short while through the woods, you will reach the first of the steps. From here you simply go up. At points the steps will end and you will think it's over, but then the steps return, getting steeper in the process. Then when you think you are about to suffer death by steps, there are some more.

You do eventually reach the top. Sort of. When you reach a gate on the right, go through it, for a lovely view down to the right. This isn't the top yet. There is a little more uphill to reach the Box Hill viewpoint with a lovely far reaching view across the Surrey Hills and to Dorking down below.

This still isn't the top.

Now continue up the hill, across the Olympic road, and into the woods on the other side. Now you're at the top.

Box wood

In the woods there is a junction with wooden signposts pointing along the left trail for the Box Hill walk. Follow this.

This next bit is quite lovely through the woods. Very easy to follow. After about 500m, look out for a log walkway type thing to the left leading to a small trail. Follow this.

This next section is a bit more off-piste. Narrow trail with some overgrowth. Sometimes you might need to crouch to get under the tree branches, and push your way through bush. It's not too aggressive though.

At the end you will reach a stile, leading to the outside, with a stunning view across the hills.

You should see a big hill ahead. You will walk up that next.

More hills

Out of the woods and over the stile, it's straight downhill and across the Olympic road.

Walking down this bit is a little precarious. It's steep and not very grippy, particularly in the rain. You might be best walking down this bit sideways.

Once you reach the bottom of the hill, and the curve in the road, stay on this main trail. It will take you uphill a little, then when it splits, take the right one and continue going up. This will lead you up and through some more trees.

When you reach a main trail, cross straight over it and walk uphill a bit more. Continue going up the grass to reach the top, where you will have another lovely view.

Everything about this spot is perfect… except the noise. The road noise is quite aggressive here. Shame.

Walk back to the steps

There is a big white trail on this hill. Turn left to follow it up. When you reach the junction, take the right trail. You will now make your way under woodland again. Make sure to keep to the main trail, as there are a few others leading off this one which will try to confuse you.

Keep going and you will reach a very interesting grave.

"Major Peter Labelliere: A 75-year-old eccentric resident of Dorking buried here, head downwards. 11th July 1800."

I've since looked into this, and apparently his name is spelt wrong, and he really died in June.

Also, his body is a few meters away from the stone. Maybe this was all on purpose, you know, due to being eccentric and stuff.

Now continue along this trail to reach the woods. These are the woods from earlier on in the walk. The woods with all the steps.

When you reach the steps, head down them.

The stepping stones

At the bottom, when you reach the junction, continue straight, following the direction for the stepping stones. When you get to them, you may hit some traffic. People like to stand on them to take photos. Blocking the way.

If the stones are underwater, you can take a trail on the right here, following the river to reach the bridge. If you managed to cross the stepping stones, on the other side, the right trail will lead you along the river towards the memorial bridge, and from there, walk back the way you came to the station.

If you parked in the car park down here, stay straight over the stones and they will lead you back to it.

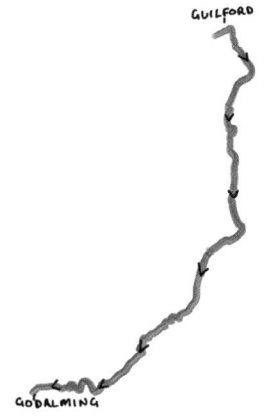

WALK 12

Guildford to Godalming along the River Wey

This is a nice and simple river walk taking you through a gap at the base of the Surrey Hills. What I mean by simple, is you don't need a map to navigate your way, and it's not too long.

Basically, it's a lovely walk to do if you don't have tons of energy and just want to switch off, or if you are new to hiking. If you do want to make it longer though, the River Wey actually runs for 20 miles, starting from Weybridge. For me, that's too long to walk straight along a river or canal. I'd get bored. But if that's your vibe, then I'm all for it.

The River Wey actually has some interesting history, which we will get to a bit later. It is also referred to as the Wey Navigation, or sometimes the Wey and Godalming navigation.

You can close your eyes and pretend you are somewhere exotic.

WHAT TO EXPECT

From the station you'll make your way to the river, but only for a short section, before a bit of road, actually a long bit of road, before returning back to the river which you'll now follow all the way to Godalming. There are some nice looking houses on the other side at first, then you'll cross over a wooden bridge. You're not allowed to jump off it, but in the summer you'll definitely see kids doing just that.

Over the bridge there is an optional hill, which will give you a lovely view over the treetops. But as I said, it's optional.

Going forward you'll pass by a few locks, which you might get to see at work. With the water being released, it sounds like a waterfall, so you can close your eyes and pretend you are somewhere exotic.

There is the occasional road crossing, but nothing aggressive, and narrowboats here and there. Most of the way is lined with trees, and rugged dirt trail, then when you reach Godalming you'll walk through the Phillips Memorial Park which has much more neat and tidy vibes.

FUN FACT:

The River Wey is the first river in Britain to be made navigable, and was used to transport goods to and from London and the River Thames. The section between Weybridge and Guildford came first. 12 locks were built and ready for use in 1653. About 100 years later, four locks were built between Guildford and Godalming.

In the 1800's, when railways started to appear, trade moved away from the rivers. With less trade, meant less money. Less money meant that the navigations couldn't be maintained. The Godalming Navigation was first to go, and by the early 1900's was derelict. The rest of the Wey Navigation remained a working waterway until the late 1960s.

DIRECTORY

LOGISTICS:

Start/Finish: Guildford Station, Godalming Station. Surrey.
Difficulty: Easy.
Type: Point to point.
Route Distance: 6 miles/9.5 km.
Time: A bit over 2h.

HOW TO GET THERE:

Direct train from London Waterloo and Clapham Junction to Guildford in 40 min – 50 min. You should buy a return ticket to Godalming, then get off one (or sometimes two) stops early at Guildford to start the walk.

COMING BY CAR:

Farnham Road car park by Guildford Station, GU2 7NP. Pay and display, card payment. Crown Court car park in Godalming, GU7 1HR, RingGo app payment. You can then get the train back at the end.

ELEVATION GAIN:

Flat.

TERRAIN:

Dirt trail, mud, road. No stiles.

DOG FRIENDLY:

Yes. Never seen livestock.

PHONE SIGNAL:

Yes.

PUBLIC TOILETS:

Yes. Both Guildford and Godalming stations have toilets.

IDEAL TIME OF YEAR:

It's particularly good in autumn, with all the autumn tree vibes. I personally avoid summer as it gets very busy. However, if you like river dips then summer would be good for that.

OPTION TO SHORTEN THE WALK:

Yes. At a bit under 3 miles, at the first road crossing, if you turn left onto the road you will reach Shalford which has a train station.

WHERE TO EAT?

Plenty of options in both Guildford and Godalming. Here are a few suggestions.

CAFE AND COFFEE:

Guildford

- Frida's Coffee House (by the river/ dog friendly).

Godalming

- Daisy Sandwiches (at the station).
- Thyme for Tea (dog friendly).
- The Godalming Food Company (dog friendly).

PUB:

Guildford

• The White House (by the river/ dog friendly).

Godalming

• The Richmond Arms (dog friendly).

FOR SUPPLIES:

Lots of supermarket options in Guildford. Waitrose and Sainsbury's in Godalming.

TIPS/OTHER THINGS TO KNOW

- You are never that far from a road or railway. So for a lot of the walk, you will hear the sound of trains and cars. Some sections are pretty peaceful, for some it's a faint background noise, and others it's quite loud.
- It will be a bit muddy after rain, so I do recommend hiking boots. During very dry summer periods, you could get away with trainers.
- No benches at all along the route, until you reach Godalming.

Just past the bridge, you will pass some steps to the right, leading up to a WWII pillbox.

ROUTE DESCRIPTION

So, I know I said you don't need any navigation skills for this walk. That's not completely true. You need to figure out the first bit out of Guildford, which is a bit confusing.

Out of the station, find your way to the underpass, which is to the right, past the bike storage.

Turn right at the other end, and then follow the road around and down to the river, where you turn right (river to your left).

This will lead you to a bridge and the White House pub. At the bridge, walk down to the river on the side next to the pub. Continue along, through a car park, and then cross the river at the next bridge.

There is another bridge straight after. Go over it, and keep going until you reach the main road.

At the main road turn right. This bit of road goes on for longer than is desirable and is very loud.

Past a car park and a pub, you should reach a green to your right. Here there are three trails, you want to take the nearest one to the river. Finally, you can walk away from the road.

You will also get a view of St Catherine's Church on a hill across the field.

Walk along the River Wey

Ok, now you are properly on the River Wey, and the walk is all simple from here. It's quite calming, getting away from the very busy road.

Back in the olden days when the river was used to transport goods, it wasn't the peaceful escape from the city which it is today. It meant business. Crew urgently trying to get their goods to the city, to catch the London tides.

You will walk under some trees with their hanging branches, with a view to some riverside houses on the other side. To the left of you is a big field. This used to be used for farming.

During the winter months, they used to raise the level of the River Wey to flood the field on purpose. It would help keep the grass warm during the winter. Then come spring, they would lower the water level to get the field ready for farming again.

Keep going to reach the bridge, then cross over it and turn left.

Walk up the hill for the views?

Over the bridge. You will see orange ground ahead to the right. Go up it if you'd like to see some views across the treetops to the hills in the distance. Just be aware, it's fairly steep and rugged, and the ground becomes sand. It's a bit slippy. It's also not essential. It's just to have a look, and you will need to come back down after.

Walk to St Catherine's Lock

The next section of the walk is easy, along a wide dirt path. With a mix of under trees and open air walking.

You will also walk past a roller thing on the river bend. Back in the day, they were to help barge boats get around the corners of the river.

Keep going and you will reach St Catherine's Lock. You will be able to see the difference in the water levels between the two sides which is interesting.

> **FUN FACT:**
> St Catherine's Lock was opened in 1764 and is the shallowest lock on the Wey.

Walk to the railway bridge and war pillbox

After St Catherine's Lock, the route stays open air, with fields to the side. Then as you walk towards and under the railway bridge, it becomes more tree lined again.

Just past the bridge, you will pass some steps to the right, leading up to a WWII pillbox. This pillbox was one of the last lines of defence protecting the capital.

Walk to Broadford Bridge and the boats

Keep walking along the river, and things go from tree cover, back to openness, as you pass some riverside houses to reach Broadford Bridge.

This is a car crossing bridge, so once it's safe to do so, cross over to join the trail on the other side, as it leads you to a nice collection of narrowboats.

Walk to Instead Lock

I find that for this section of the walk, the car noise goes on for a little longer than is comfortable. Due to the road running parallel to the river, the noise is pretty loud until you pass by and under the next bridge.

Under the bridge, the muddy dirt path continues (and the road noise dissipates), and you will walk past a Wey Navigation river split. There is a sign here pointing which way boats and river traffic should go. Like for cars on roads.

You will walk over a cute wooden bridge, not to cross to the other side of the river, but to cross a little offshoot coming onto the river. When on the bridge, there is a gap to the right, and you can see a hidden home with a lawn leading to their own bit of river.

Keep going and you will soon reach Instead Lock.

Walk to Catteshall Lock

You will then walk past a cute bridge, and things become a bit more open again. With a view to the tree covered hills across the river, and a little secluded looking home in the distance.

This bit can be particularly muddy.

The trail then travels around a bend, under more trees and then back to the open views. You will then approach a section where the trail is lined with fence, and houses on the other side.

Past the houses, and another cute bridge, you will reach another concentration of houses. This time with lots of narrowboats.

Just past the boats is Catteshall Lock.

Walk to Godalming

At this point, there is a sense that the walk is nearly over. Across the field to the right are lots of houses, and a peak to a church hidden within some trees. It also becomes significantly louder with the car noise.

Don't write it off yet though, it gets pretty as you enter Godalming, and unlike a lot of walks, you don't have to navigate your way through a town. The river basically leads you right to the station.

Once you reach the bridge in Godalming the whole vibe of the trail changes. In fact, it becomes less of a trail, and more of a civilised path.

Cross over the bridge, and pick up the path on the other side. This takes you along the river as it runs through the Phillips Memorial Park.

It's quite pretty in here, and the view across the river is lovely. To a green, and houses nestled within the trees on the other side. Maybe some cows and swans.

Keep on the path as it winds you alongside the river, past a church and graveyard.

When you reach the road, across the other side to the left is a small trail leading behind some houses. Walk along this, then at the road on the other side, go left, and you should see the Godalming Station car park ahead.

Guildford to Godalming along the River Wey

PUBLIC TRANSPORT

The Chilterns are so close to London, and all these walks you can get to in under one hour by train using the following routes.

London Marylebone – Chiltern Railways

London Euston – London North Western Railway (LNR)

London Paddington – Great Western Railway

WALK 13
Wendover, Coombe Hill, and Chequers
7 miles

WALK 14
Henley-on-Thames to Aston and Stonor park
8 miles

WALK 15
Tring to Ivinghoe Beacon
9 miles

WALK 16
Henley-on-Thames to Greys court
8 miles

CHILTERNS NATIONAL LANDSCAPE

The Chiltern Hills are an area of beautiful countryside located just north west of London.

Home to some of the most beautiful towns and villages in Britain, rolling green hills, woodland, chalk hill figures, Iron Age hill forts, country estates, and a little bit of the River Thames. You can even do walks to take you from one beautiful quaint town or village to another.

It's so beautiful that it's been made official. It's a designated AONB (now National Landscape). Sort of. Some of it was designated in 1965, and then this was extended in 1990, to now cover 324 square miles of countryside spanning across Oxfordshire, Buckinghamshire, Hertfordshire and Bedfordshire… all the shires.

But it doesn't stop there. Talks are underway to extend the boundary to cover even more of the Chilterns.

As you go further south, the Chilterns merge into the North Wessex National Landscape, and the Ridgeway National Trail runs through them both. At 87 miles, it's a long distance walking trail, and is the oldest road in Britain, dating back to prehistoric times.

WALK 13

Wendover, Coombe Hill, and Chequers

This walk takes you up some big hills for what I would say are the best views across the Chilterns.

Views to rival Ivinghoe Beacon, which tends to claim that title. At around 260m, you will be at the second highest point in the Chilterns. Apparently, on a clear day you can see as far as the Cotswolds.

There is a nice variety on this one, with Wendover, a historic market town at the start. It's known as the gateway to the Chilterns. You'll definitely want to spend a moment wandering around here at the end of the walk. It's even said that Oliver Cromwell spent the night in the Red Lion Inn.

I will explain the whole route, but best take a map just in case.

WHAT TO EXPECT

Out of the station it's a short walk to reach the trail where you'll reach the first hill. The hills and views take up the first half of the walk. Bacombe Hill, Coombe Hill and Beacon Hill. Although, it's not as hard work as it sounds. The first two hills are sort of connected, so you only have one big uphill there. The third hill is optional. I will explain later.

The second half of the walk is characterised by fields and woodland. Dense woodland, which you could easily get lost in. I will explain the whole route, but best take a map just in case.

FUN FACT:
In 1214, a market charter was awarded by King John, and markets have since been held in Wendover to this day.

You will also walk around the Chequers Estate. The Prime Minister's country home, with an unusual amount of signage warning you not to enter.

DIRECTORY

LOGISTICS:

Start/Finish: Wendover Station, Buckinghamshire.
Difficulty: Moderate.
Type: Circular.
Route Distance: 7 miles/11 km.
Time: 3–4h.

HOW TO GET THERE:

Direct trains from London Marylebone to Wendover on Chiltern Railways. Journey time 50min.

COMING BY CAR:

The Witcher Pavilion car park in Wendover HP22 6EF. Or the Coombe Hill car park HP17 0UR. It's National Trust, so free for members. If you park here, head over to the memorial, and you can start the trail from there.

ELEVATION GAIN:

372m/1220ft.

TERRAIN:

Lots of mud, dirt trail, more mud, grass, small amount of road. No stiles.

DOG FRIENDLY:

Yes. However, some loose cows are about.

PHONE SIGNAL:

Yes.

PUBLIC TOILETS:

Only at Wendover Station.

IDEAL TIME OF YEAR:

Autumn for all the autumn colours. Preferably not after a lot of rain due to the mud.

OPTION TO SHORTEN THE WALK:

Only if you miss out something. A nice option would be to walk to Coombe Hill and back. That's just under 2 miles one way.

WHERE TO EAT?

Only one place along the route, but plenty of options in Wendover.

CAFE AND COFFEE:

Wendover

- Crumbs Cafe (dogs allowed in outside seating).
- Whitewaters Deli Cafe (dogs allowed in outside seating).

On the walk

- 5 miles: Buckmoorend Farm shop (dogs allowed in outside seating).

PUB:

Wendover

- Shoulder of Mutton (just outside the station/ 17th Century/ dog friendly).
- The Red Lion Coaching Inn (17th Century/ dog friendly).

FOR SUPPLIES:

Sweeney's supermarket.

TIPS/OTHER THINGS TO KNOW

- Hiking boots definitely.
- It can get a little windy at the top of the hills.
- Can be very muddy particularly after rain.
- With the HS2 being built, the start of the walk out of Wendover is subject to change. It will be easy to navigate though if you have a map, and can see all the trail options to get you up to Bacombe Hill, and then you can continue following the route description.

You are already uphill, so you've done the hard work.

ROUTE DESCRIPTION

Out of the station, turn right to reach the main road, then right again over the bridge. Now, there is a quicker way to get to the first hill, but if the HS2 is still in the way, you'll have to take a slightly longer route. Only slightly longer though.

A short way after the bridge, you should see a trail across the road on the left. Take that trail and follow it around the edge of a field under some pylons, which you should hear crackling. Slightly unnerving.

At the time of writing, the construction site will be to your right. Someway along the trail, some barriers (like for trains) are controlling the walkers vs construction vehicles. I find it quite novel.

Continue along the trail to reach the country road, where you turn right. A short way up, look out for a trail sign on the right, directing you into an uphill field. Where there may or may not be cows or a bull.

You need to walk through the field to the top left corner. I don't like to take any chances with the cows, so skirt around the edge. With the barbed wire fence as an escape.

Through the gate at the top, continue across the trail straight through the woods, going uphill some more, and you will soon exit the woods to reach the hilltop. This is where the magic begins. The views.

This is Bacombe Hill. You don't need to hang around too long, as they are about to get better.

Walk across Bacombe Hill

Follow the grass trail to the left (at 10 o'clock). This will lead you between bushes and trees, before opening up to even more incredible views.

Continue on, through some more trees, then at the junction with the trail signpost, follow the direction straight across for the Ridgeway.

Coombe Hill

You are already uphill, so you've done the hard work. You just need to go up a little more to reach the top of Coombe Hill.

As you approach, you will see the Coombe Hill Monument ahead.

The Coombe Hill Monument was built in 1904 in memory of 148 men from Buckinghamshire, who served and gave their lives during the South African War 1899–1902.

Up here you have a view across the Aylesbury Vale (and maybe the Cotswolds if you squint).

Straight across from the monument (from the direction you arrived here on), you should see a big hill ahead. That's the next hill. Beacon Hill.

Walk to Beacon Hill

Past the monument, turn left, so you are walking along the edge of the hilltop, with Beacon Hill to your right.

When you reach the fence at the end, stay on this side of it, and turn right.

It's now a very very steep downhill. There is absolutely no way you will be able to walk down this hill on the official trail without slipping, but you can use the grass to the left which offers some grip… and I still can't guarantee you won't slip.

Don't worry, you won't have to walk back up this for the way back. The hill you will do, is only a little bit steep.

Keep going all the way down to reach the road at the bottom, then turn right. Past the cottages there is a trail to the left, which will take you across a crop field.

On the other side of the field, when you reach the country lane, turn right to reach the main road. Ahead of you will be a thatched roofed cottage, and St Peter's and St Paul's Church.

Turn left at the road, and a short way along is the trail back into some fields on the left. As you enter, you will be faced with Beacon Hill straight ahead. Now walk towards it. The uphill starts here. Gentle at first.

When you reach the gate, you can choose whether or not you want to walk up the final steep incline to the summit. You can't go anywhere up the top, it's a dead end, so you will need to come back down anyway.

Walk to Chequers

The trail skirts around the right of the hill, and there is a trail sign here in case you aren't sure. It starts off grassy and less obvious, but you will soon be led onto a proper trail, into the trees.

Through the trees there are some rugged wooden steps. I say some, there are actually lots. Lots of steps. You do have more wonderful views to the right though, across the treetops.

At the top, walk straight across the field and into the next woodland.

Keep going through the woods to the next gate.

The woods on your left are part of the Chequers estate. I don't actually know this for sure, as it doesn't say it is, but there are about 100 (not really) signs warning you not to enter. Something about it being protected under the Serious Organised Crime and Police Act. I wonder why there is no fence?

Anyway, go through the gate ahead, and turn left to walk along the edge of the field. There might be cows in here, but it's ok because you can stick to the edge. The edge is also where they choose to do their poos. Follow the edge of the field around to the left, and you will reach a fence, gate, and trail sign. Follow the Ridgeway direction through the gate.

To your left is a big field, with a manor house nestled within the trees on the other side. That is Chequers.

My first time here I stood taking lots of photos. Maybe too many. I then wondered if they were watching and would get suspicious so I ceased and moved on.

Further along, the trail will curve to the right, then look out for a missable gate on the left hidden in the bushes. There should be a trail signpost here.

Head through it and down across the field. This is still Chequers. In fact, you must not venture off this trail as police with police dogs are watching… or so the signs say.

At the bottom, go through the gate, and straight across the road then through the next gate, then follow the trail up the field which will lead you to the road.

Walk through the woods

Across the road, there is the Buckmoorend Farm shop if you fancy popping in. To continue on, the trail is to the left.

You're going to be following the Ridgeway trail for a bit. I'll tell you when to change.

Following the trail, take the right at the first fork, then just continue uphill through the woods. This is Goodmerhill Wood. It's a somewhat steep uphill, but not too bad. At some point it does level out.

You need to keep following the Ridgeway trail at the junctions, then you will turn off at the third left. It's about 1/2 a mile in. There is only a small trail sign at this junction, but there might be some arrows on the trees.

It's another uphill here, now through Fugsdon Wood, to reach the road.

Pick up the trail directly opposite the road. There are actually two trails here. Left is more direct, but more confusing, so take the right one. It's the more obvious one.

When you reach the junction at the top (yes, you are walking uphill some more), turn left. You are now walking through High Scrubs. No more uphill…. for now.

When you reach a big junction, the trail sign will tell you to turn left. Ignore that, and follow the trail as it curves to the right. It might start to feel like you are going the wrong way. Trust the process.

For the rest of the walk through the woods, you will be walking in this direction. At times the trail is obvious, and others not so much. Remember, at any junctions, stay in this direction.

You are now in Upper Bacombe.

Walk back to Wendover

If you don't get lost, you will then exit the woods with a lovely view down to some trees below, and hills in the distance. Keep following this main trail as it takes you down and through a mix of open and tree lined trail, with a sneaky hill thrown in.

You should eventually reach the road. If you turn right, you will be where you were from the start, so can retrace your steps. I will guide you though, if you aren't sure.

Follow the road down, keeping an eye out for a gate hidden in the bushes to the left. Go through the gate, and turn right. Now follow this trail (at the time of writing through a construction site).

At the other end, follow the trail as it curves to the left around the perimeter of the field and around the pylons with their crackling noises, and you will reach the road. Wendover and the station will be to the right.

Wendover

Now explore Wendover. It's a very small town, right next to the station, so you won't have to do too much walking. If you head to the square, there is an information board telling you all the history, and about the buildings around you.

Something quite interesting, it's rumoured that Oliver Cromwell, and Robert Louis Stevenson have spent the night in the Red Lion.

Also, the largest windmill in England is here. However, its sails have been removed and it's now a private home.

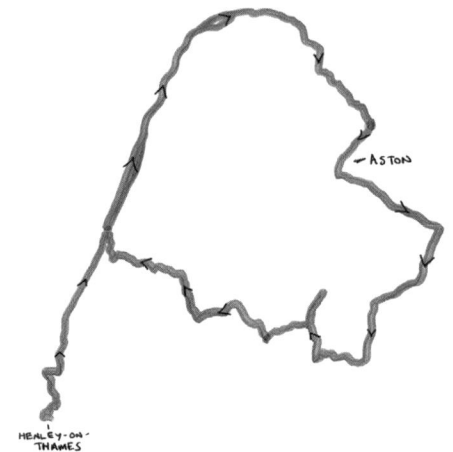

WALK 14

Henley-on-Thames to Aston and Stonor Park

This walk features a riverside path, impressive houses, a pub, white deer, hills, woodland, and views. But of course, I can't not mention where it begins.

The charming Henley-on-Thames. Frequently voted one of the most beautiful towns in England, and one the best places to live in the English countryside, and that I can see. With its historic buildings, independent shops, and a thriving food scene, all with a riverside setting.

I would describe the walk as tidy, clean, calm, posh. Think manicured grass and swans. Everything is just so neat. Almost too neat. Not quite my usual rugged roughness, but I do enjoy this one. Easy to get to from London, simple to follow, and overall it's a great day out, as after you finish, you could spend a good amount of time wandering around Henley.

Everything is just so neat.
Almost too neat.
Not quite my usual rugged roughness.

WHAT TO EXPECT

The walk starts out along the river, and you may see rowers training, with the odd kayaker here and there. There are a few massive houses on the other side of the river. So you can admire from afar and imagine what it would be like to live there.

After about three miles, you turn inland through the tiny village of Aston with a pub.

Then things change a bit, and you will be walking on the side of a hill with a lovely view down to the river and the hills beyond, before reaching Stonor Park.

It's not marked on Google Maps, as this is a private park with a walking trail through it. What's special about this park is it's a deer park with white deer. Yes. White deer.

FUN FACT:

Henley-on-Thames is home to The Royal Regatta, one of the longest running sporting events in the country.

After Stonor Park, the vibe changes a little as you circle back. A bit more rugged, through some woods, and lovely views across the hills.

DIRECTORY

LOGISTICS:

Start/Finish: Henley-on-Thames Station, Oxfordshire.
Difficulty: Easy.
Type: Circular.
Route Distance: 8 miles/13 km.
Time: 2–3h.

HOW TO GET THERE:

Get a train from London Paddington to Henley. There is a change at Twyford. Journey time 40–50 min.

COMING BY CAR:

Mill Meadow car park, RG9 1BE. Southfields car park, RG9 1BJ. Both in Henley, then head to the river to start the walk.

ELEVATION GAIN:

334m/1096ft.

TERRAIN:

Tidy path, grass, dirt trail, a bit of road. No stiles.

DOG FRIENDLY:

Yes. But on a lead through Stonor Park, and for some sections on the route back.

PHONE SIGNAL:

Yes.

PUBLIC TOILETS:

There are a few in Henley.

IDEAL TIME OF YEAR:

Autumn for the colourful leaves, spring for the flowers. If you don't like lots of people, then avoid summer.

OPTION TO SHORTEN THE WALK:

Yes. Walk to Aston for a pub lunch, then turn back the way you came. This will be about 6 miles, and cuts out all the hills.

WHERE TO EAT?

One pub along the route, then tons of options in Henley, here are a few suggestions.

CAFE AND COFFEE:

Henley
- Spoon Cafe (dog friendly).
- Hot Gossip (dog friendly).
- Geo Cafe (dog friendly).

PUB:

Henley
- The Angle on the Bridge (dog friendly).

On the walk
- 3 miles: The Flower Pot, Aston (dog friendly).

FOR SUPPLIES:

Sainsbury's Local and Waitrose.

TIPS/OTHER THINGS TO KNOW

- Check what events are on before heading out i.e. the Royal Regatta, boat races etc. It will be particularly busy on those days. If you don't like lots of people, then avoid these times. If you want to be a part of it, then go along and have fun.
- You're not guaranteed to see the deer. I haven't seen them on every trip.
- Stonor Park is a private park, so you must keep to the trail. It's not the kind of place you can go for a picnic, or to play frisbee.
- For part of the second half of the walk, you will be near a busy road, so you will hear it. If you don't fancy that, then when you reach Stonor Park, turn back the way you came.
- If you plan to just walk to Stonor Park and back, then trainers are fine for this walk. If you do the full circular, then wear hiking boots.

*I wonder if this place
has ever seen mud?
It feels too posh for that.*

ROUTE DESCRIPTION

From the station, it's a short walk to the river. Turn right, then right at the end, and you will reach it.

From there, walk over to the bridge and cross over it. This bit can be a little congested, with everyone else arriving on the train.

Over the bridge, turn left and along the riverside path. It's all very civilised and neat here. There is a big green where rowers are often prepping to get into the water. In their funky leggings and posh accents.

The path continues on, past some rowing clubs, with a view to the hills ahead in the distance. As you get further away from Henley, the path turns to dirt and grass. Still very neat and clean though. I wonder if this place has ever seen mud? It feels too posh for that.

It's somewhere along here that the grand houses on the other side of the river start to appear. You can imagine what it would be like to live in one.

When you reach Hambledon Lock, stay on this side of the river, but you can have a little walk over the lock to see the view.

Walk to Aston

When you reach the end of the path, with a little pier and another grand house on the other side, leave the river heading right, towards Aston.

It's a short walk to reach the village, which consists of some houses and one pub.

Walk to Stonor Park

Continue up the road, then take a left following the signs for the Thames Path. This will lead you past a couple of houses (at the first junction, right is someone's drive, so take the left) and then along the side of the hill, where everything opens up. You'll have a wonderful view down to the river and the hills on the other side.

If you know me, you know I am a view person, so it's a nice change from being down on the river.

Top tip: Look up the hill to the right. You will see some sort of sculpture.

Keep going and you will reach Stonor Park through some black metal gates. In Stonor Park, you need to keep to the trail. There are a few signs warning you of this. Keep going all the way to reach the big trail signpost, and turn right here, to head up to the woodland. Hopefully you will see the deer.

The trail disappears a little, but continue straight through the woods and out the other side. You will soon be on path again.

As you go further into the park, the more it opens up, and it's pretty incredible. You wouldn't know it from the trail you arrived on. It's massive, with a grand valley and sweeping views.

The grass is also immaculate. You might see some groundsmen driving around, tending to things. You will then reach a signpost pointing right, down into the valley and up the other side, where you will then get more incredible views.

The whole vibe will change now, so if you would prefer to keep things as is (neat and tidy) then turn back here.

Circle back to Henley

At the top, through the gate, turn left to walk along the drive.

Then just before the houses and road, turn right to walk along the perimeter of a crop field. At the end, turn left through the gate, and this will lead you around to Aston Road where it joins the main road.

Turn right here along Aston Road. If you follow this road all the way to the end, you will reach Aston with the pub. It's a country lane road without walkway, but speed limit is just 30 miles per hour, not the national speed limit as country roads tend to be.

For this walk though, as you reach the last house, turn left onto the trail through the hedges. At the next road, cross over to pick up the trail on the other side, and turn right. You will now make your way through a mass of bushes and trees. The rugged part.

At the end, you will exit at a farm. Keep straight along the top of the hill.

You might see some llamas (or the other one, alpacas) here.

Last time I was here, it was three months until Christmas day, and the llamas (or alpacas) were with all the turkeys. I stood to watch the llamas, and the turkeys came running after me. If there wasn't a fence between us, I'm pretty sure I would have been engulfed by turkey. Like some sort of horror movie. Turkey attack. They were making so much noise, I wondered if the farmer might come and tell me off, so I left quickly.

Continue to the end, through the bushes, to reach the road. Turn right here.

A few minutes walk along, just past the house, turn left onto the trail.

You will be in the woods briefly, with wonderful views to the right, and then walk down along the edge of a field, following the view, and you will start to see the river again. You are very close to Henley now, and when you reach the bottom of this field, you have two options.

Option 1. Turn left to continue along the field to reach Henley.

Option 2. Turn right to reach the road.

Taking Option 2, at the road, turn right, then a short way along you can turn left past the boat house to get back onto the river. From there, make your way back to Henley.

WALK 15

Tring to Ivinghoe Beacon via Aldbury

This walk takes you along the Ridgeway, a long distance National Trail, to reach Ivinghoe Beacon, the site of an Iron Age hill fort. Evidence of human activity has been found here, dating back to the Bronze Age. It's also a fantastic viewpoint, and at 233m high, you can see all of England. Ok, you can't actually see all of England, just a few counties and the Whipsnade White Lion, a white chalk hill figure dating back to 1933. It was designed by R.B. Brook-Greaves to advertise the zoo.

This walk doesn't go to the zoo, but it does go to a quaint chocolate box village with some pubs.

There's a bit of woodland, and it's a bit hilly, but the views make up for the hills.

WHAT TO EXPECT

It's a short walk from Tring Station to reach the Ridgeway Trail, which you will follow all the way up to Ivinghoe Beacon for about 3 miles. There's a bit of woodland, and it's a bit hilly, but the views make up for the hills.

You will then walk along a ridge which, funnily enough, is not the Ridgeway National Trail (the Ridgeway ends at Ivinghoe Beacon), with a view ahead to the White Lion chalk figure.

Next you will loop back, through mostly woodland, but also some fields, and a few more hills, to reach the village of Aldbury with thatched roofed cottages, and optional pub stop. From there it's just a short walk, across some fields and along a dirt trail, to get back to the station.

FUN FACT:

A lot of filming has gone on around these parts…

Ivinghoe Beacon was in Harry Potter and Star Wars, the White Lion was in Merlin. Aldbury has been on screen quite a lot too, in Bridget Jones' Diary, The Avengers, and Midsomer Murders to name a few. A funny one is, Aldbury was used in the initial advertisement for the National Lottery, despite the fact that the village shop was unable to sell tickets.

DIRECTORY

LOGISTICS:

Start/Finish: Tring Station, Hertfordshire.
Difficulty: Moderate.
Type: Circular.
Route Distance: 9 miles/14.5 km.
Time: 3–4h.

HOW TO GET THERE:

Direct trains from London Euston to Tring. West Midlands Railway. Journey time 40 min.

COMING BY CAR:

A few free parking options near Ivinghoe Beacon – Ivinghoe Beacon car park LU7 9EJ, Steps Hill car park, Pitstone Hill car park. You can then freestyle the walk or you can still follow the same route starting from Ivinghoe Beacon, but in the route description, at the end, take a right at the Ridgeway sign instead of continuing straight to reach the road. The Ridgeway will then lead you back to Ivinghoe Beacon.

ELEVATION GAIN:

457m/1499ft.

TERRAIN:

Grassy trails, dirt trails, some mud if it has rained, a bit of road. No stiles.

DOG FRIENDLY:

Yes, but there are some loose sheep about.

PHONE SIGNAL:

Yes.

PUBLIC TOILETS:

No, but there are places to eat at Aldbury which will have toilets.

IDEAL TIME OF YEAR:

Anytime, avoiding rain and high wind. There is a lot of woodland, so autumn is nice.

OPTION TO SHORTEN THE WALK:

Yes, if you skip out Aldbury. From the station, walk to Ivinghoe Beacon, then come back the way you came. This will be 7 miles.

WHERE TO EAT?

The only places to eat are in Aldbury.

CAFE AND COFFEE:

Aldbury
- The Church Farm Cafe (dog friendly).
- Poppies Cafe (dog friendly).

PUB:

Aldbury
- Greyhound Inn (dog friendly).
- The Trooper (dog friendly).

FOR SUPPLIES:

Village store in Aldbury.

TIPS/OTHER THINGS TO KNOW

- Ivinghoe Beacon is quite exposed, and can get quite windy up there.
- The route to Ivinghoe Beacon, and the surrounding area can get busy during summer weekends, but past there, the number of people tends to drop off. Aldbury might also be busy at the end.
- The White Lion wasn't looking quite as chalky on my most recent visit. It was actually restored with over 800 tons of chalk in 2017, but nature seems to be reclaiming the land a bit.
- Hiking boots recommended.

*If it's a busy day,
you will see 'ant people'
in the distance.*

ROUTE DESCRIPTION

From the station, walk through the car park and take a right along the road. There is a field on the right here which you can walk along if you don't want to walk on the roadside.

A few minutes walk along, take the second left, and through the gate. There is signage here for the Ridgeway, which you will be following all the way to Ivinghoe Beacon now.

Next it's a gentle walk uphill, with gorgeous views to the right.

At the next junction with signage, go left and you will now follow this trail for a while, mostly under tree cover, with occasional views to the left.

As the trail curves to the right, there is a short but steep uphill, and things open up, with a strategically placed bench where you can sit to admire the views. The openness is only brief, as the trail continues up and back under tree cover.

A bit further along, you will reach some Ridgeway signage with wooden steps to the left. Take those steps, and continue going up.

At this point, you will have been walking uphill a bit, it's mostly gentle with some short steeper bits.

All the views

You will reach a junction where to the left is a tree with a rope swing. I haven't tried it out, but it looks like it could be fun. Don't go left here though, instead continue straight on, and out of the woods.

This is where the main views begin.

The trail continues straight and up and then along the hilltop, with some undulations, and wonderful views all around. All the way in the distance you will see Ivinghoe Beacon. You are now heading straight towards that.

If you look to the left, try to spot the Pitstone Windmill. It's black in the middle of a field.

At the car park, walk straight through and across the road, and head towards the next big hill. If it's a busy day, you will see 'ant people' in the distance. As you make your way up the big hill, it will curve around to the left with the valley below. The view is pretty spectacular here.

When you reach a gate, don't go through it. Stay on this trail, and you should reach a viewpoint bench overlooking where you have just come from.

Walk to Ivinghoe Beacon

If you stand in front of the bench, facing it, take the trail past it to the left. This will take you through some bushes and gates, as you gently undulate up and down some more.

You will soon be able to see Ivinghoe Beacon ahead again.

When you reach the road, the Ridgeway sign doesn't quite point the correct way. There are two main trails across the road. The sign points to the right one. Don't do that. Take the left one which is straight across. This will take you on your final uphill (or two) to reach the top of Ivinghoe Beacon.

Pictures don't do the views up here any justice. On a clear day you can see across multiple counties. There might also be some kite flyers and little toy aeroplanes.

Whipsnade White Lion

You should see the ridge to the right. Ironically, this isn't the Ridgeway National Trail. That's finished now. Follow this, and you will soon get a view ahead to the Whipsnade White Lion.

The first time I did this walk, I had no idea I would see the lion. I'd seen photos of it online, but didn't know where it was. So it was a very pleasant surprise seeing it here.

During the second world war, it had to be covered up to prevent it being used for navigation by enemy aircraft. On the flip side, in 1981 as part of the Whipsnade Zoo's 50th anniversary, the White Lion was illuminated with 750 lightbulbs.

Keep going along the ridge, with stunning views down either side, and the lion ahead. Then when you reach the end with a gate, don't go through it, but instead turn right to walk down the hill. You should see a long white trail cutting across the bottom. That's where you will walk next.

Walk to Aldbury

Follow the white trail to the right, towards the hill and trees ahead.

When you go through the gate, turn left, then take the right at the fork which comes quite soon after.

At the next fork, stay straight and the trail will soon curve around to the right and up the hill. Make sure to look back for more wonderful views. I've actually spotted deer here before, down in the valley to the left, so keep an eye out for them.

At the top, go through the gate and go up a little more to reach the road. There is a green here on the left which you walk across, to reach the entrance to the woods on the left. There is a random gate in here that leads to nowhere. Ignore that, and stay on the main trail through the woods.

Keep an eye out for a junction about 1/4 of a mile along, where you turn sharply back to the right. It's very easy to miss. This will lead you up to the road.

Cross over the road, and turn left. You will now follow the road for about 1/4 of a mile. You have the option of walking in the woods next to it for a bit of it. It's quite rugged there though, and you will be forced back to the road after a short distance anyway. There is a trail next to the road, not the nicest trail mind you. It's just super narrow and surrounded by overgrown stuff. In parts almost not visible.

Tring to Ivinghoe Beacon via Aldbury

When you reach a lay-by type area, you can head straight into the woods. When you enter, turn left, then a short way along, take the first trail on the right. Keep going straight now, across any junctions, and then downhill into a potentially confusing mass of woodland.

In here, the trail will bear to the left then up on the right, to reach a gate.

Through the gate, you will leave the woods and enter a big field. Sometimes there are cows in here.

Continue along the top of the hill, then through the next gate follow the narrow trail down across the field to reach the road. Go straight across the road and into the crop field, then take the trail on a diagonal left straight through it. This will lead you through a hole in the hedge, then across another crop field, to reach the road and another gate. Go straight through this gate, and along the right edge of the field.

You will then reach another field, with a gate on the left. Go through the gate and along the fence lined trail.

At the next road, go through that gate on the other side into another field.

Yes, I know, there seems to be a lot of roads, but these are all either quiet roads, or driveways. I don't feel it spoils the walk.

Go straight across this field, with some nice looking cottages to the right, partially hidden by the trees. At the end, go through a gate, and across another field to reach the road, where you turn left.

You are now in Aldbury. You will first pass by thatched roofed cottages and Tudor facades to reach the pond in the centre, and the Greyhound Pub.

There isn't a lot here. Just general quaintness, a village store, church, and a couple of cafes and pubs.

Walk back to Tring Station

Head to the church and follow the path through the graveyard which will lead you back to the road, where you turn right. Not too far along, there is a trail on the right to take you across the field.

The farm style building ahead to the left is the Church Farm Cafe. I'm not sure you can access it from here if you want to go in. The gate seemed to be locked.

Anyway, continue past it, but remember to look back to Aldbury for the pretty views, before going onto a narrow trail through the gate on the left.

Keep going straight now, alongside a mix of bushes, hedges, and trees.

At the end, turn left, and this will lead you back to the road from the start of the walk. (If you have come by car and parked at Ivinghoe Beacon, look out for the right turning with a Ridgeway sign).

When you reach the road, turn right along it and you will reach Tring Station. If you don't want to walk right next to the road, you can walk along a trail in the field opposite.

One thing I really like about this walk is that there are regular trains back to London. There is nothing worse than arriving at a station having just missed a train, and having to wait an hour for the next one.

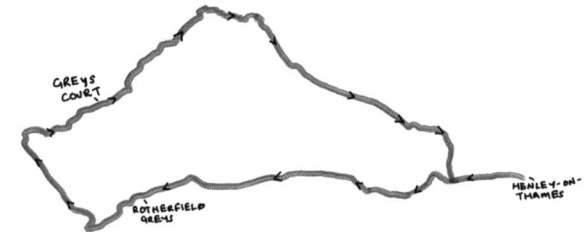

WALK 16

Henley-on-Thames to Greys Court

This walk takes you from the charming market town of Henley-on-Thames, for a good old countryside stomp across the Chiltern Hills to reach Greys Court, a Tudor country house.

There is one section of woodland on this walk which needs a special mention. Lambridge Wood. If you are a solo walker that gets a bit nervous walking alone, this might not be the walk for you. It's the kind of woods you could easily get lost in, with no clear trail. In the times I've walked through there, I've not come across a single other person, and there is a definite spooky lost in the woods feeling. They are damn impressive woods though.

This route is much quieter and more peaceful than walking along the river from Henley, which is the popular one. So it's a great way to escape the crowds.

It was pretty wild. I can't tell you how much of a difference this makes.

WHAT TO EXPECT

Out of Henley, there is a little bit of road to reach the trail, then it's a mix of woods, fields, some uphill, lovely views, and a small village with a pub to reach Greys Court. You can explore inside Greys Court or just walk straight past. You only need to pay if you want to go inside.

This is the halfway point. If you want to do this walk but don't want to walk through Lambridge Wood, then you can instead walk back the way you came.

To continue on with the circular, it's about 1/2 a mile now, before you reach the woods. What I can say though about the woods, is there are now white arrows painted on the trees guiding you through them. The first time I did this walk, there were no arrows (or I didn't see them). It was pretty wild. I can't tell you how much of a difference this makes.

FUN FACT:

Greys Court, now owned by the National Trust, was a filming location for Downton Abbey, Agatha Christie's Poirot, and Midsomer Murders.

It's about 1 mile through the woods, which doesn't sound far, but it definitely feels it when you have that lost in the woods feeling, and all you have to go by is arrows on the trees. Plus, there are trail splits where you need to follow different arrows. It feels a little bit like a game. Where's the next arrow? After this you will be in the obligatory countryside walk golf course, before finishing along residential streets to reach Henley.

DIRECTORY

LOGISTICS:

Start/Finish: Henley-on-Thames Station, Oxfordshire.
Difficulty: Easy.
Type: Circular.
Route Distance: 8 miles/13 km.
Time: 3–4h.

HOW TO GET THERE:

London Paddington to Henley-on-Thames (with a change at Twyford) on Great Western Railway. Journey time 40–50 min.

COMING BY CAR:

Mill Meadow car park, RG9 1BE. Southfields car park, RG9 1BJ. Both in Henley.

ELEVATION GAIN:

251m/823ft.

TERRAIN:

Grass, dirt trail, some road, stiles, lots of mud after rain.

DOG FRIENDLY:

Somewhat, there are a few restrictions/precautions (see tips).

PHONE SIGNAL:

Yes.

PUBLIC TOILETS:

A few in Henley, or if you go into Greys Court.

IDEAL TIME OF YEAR:

Spring for the bluebells at Greys Court, or autumn for the colourful leaves.

OPTION TO SHORTEN THE WALK:

No.

WHERE TO EAT?

A couple of options along the route, then lots to choose from in Henley. Here are a few suggestions.

CAFE AND COFFEE:

Henley

- Spoon Cafe (dog friendly).
- Hot Gossip (dog friendly).
- Bistro at the Boathouse (dogs allowed outside).

On the walk

- The Tea Room at Greys Court (dog friendly).

PUB:

Henley

- The Angle on the Bridge in Henley (dog friendly).

On the walk

- The Malters Arms, Rotherfield Greys (a bit before you reach Greys Court/ dog friendly).

FOR SUPPLIES:

Sainsbury's Local and Waitrose in Henley.

TIPS/OTHER THINGS TO KNOW

- If you want to explore around Greys Court, I would book tickets in advance. Be aware though that during busy times, they might issue a timed ticket.

- If coming with a dog, there is one field with ground nesting birds where they will need to be on a lead (you are warned when you enter), and on a lead at Greys Court. Some livestock in some fields. There are many stiles, but all have doggy sized holes. There is road walking at the start and end, then a couple of road crossings during the walk.

*Someone had told me
if you catch a falling
leaf it's good luck.*

ROUTE DESCRIPTION

From the station, head to the river. It's a right turn, then right turn at the end. Walk towards the bridge, then turn left onto the highstreet. Keep going up and along the road to the left of the clock tower.

It's now a bit of an uphill walk next to the road (you will want to get onto the right side of it at some point, as the pavement ends on this side), and further up past the houses, you should see a trail signpost on the other side of the road pointing left. So cross back over and take it.

You are still on a road, but this time one of those country lane types with no pavement and super curvy. It's not a busy road though, and leads to a school. When you reach the entrance to the school, take the trail to the right of it.

It's a bit of a woodland walk along here, with the occasional view to the open field to the right. When you reach a junction with a gate, don't go through the gate, but instead take the trail on the right. Not the trail straight ahead! It's the trail on the right, and easily missable.

This will take you out of the woods and along the middle of a valley.

The first time I did this walk, on the train out here I suddenly got anxiety out of nowhere, and felt like I was on the verge of a panic attack. I used to suffer with them. I didn't feel good. It was around this point in the walk that I felt a wash of calm run through me, and it all went away. It's just so peaceful.

Keep going, and you should start to see a cute looking house ahead. I think this must belong to a farm. There are a series of two stiles coming up. After the first one, there might be some livestock, but not too long after, the next stile takes you out of the field and along a big muddy track.

Walk to Rotherfield Greys

Keep going, and the trail will lead you to a big junction. You want to now head into the big field, ahead and slightly right. You'll know the one, as all the other trails say no entry.

At the end of the field, when the main trail curves left towards an unusual amount of no entry signs, you go right and over a stile into a field which is the one with birds' nests on the ground. Keep going straight along the edge of this field, and in the second field a little past the gate, look out for a stile to the left through the trees.

Over the stile, turn right and follow the trail as it then curves to the left uphill.

I was here once in autumn, and there was a strong gust of wind blowing the leaves off the trees. Someone had told me if you catch a falling leaf it's good luck. So I scrambled around trying to catch one. Like the Crystal Maze. I was not successful.

Keep on this trail as it levels out, and it will lead you to Rotherfield Greys village with a church and pub. You can stop at the pub of course, but to continue on the walk, take the trail to the right of the church. This leads you alongside a narrow trail between the church and hedge, and then through a couple of gates, and onto a trail between the field and hedge.

At the end through another gate, you will be in a field. The trail is grassy and almost not visible, but it leads ahead and slightly right.

Once through the gate at the other end of the field, turn right to walk along a long stretch of tree and bush tunnel.

Walk to Greys Court

At the end, cross over the road to pick up the trail on the other side, in what I'm going to call, messy woodland. This takes you to another road, where you do the same again. This time it takes you to the back of some houses, where you turn right to walk around the white walled house to reach the green.

You now want to head to the far left side of the green, where the cottages are. If you follow the perimeter around, just before the cottage, there is a trail to the left. This will lead you into some woodland.

You will come across a half fallen tree. It looks like it's about to snap and fall. But you are safe! It has already fallen, and is being held up by another big tree. So you can safely walk under it (I think).

The trail will lead you through the woods to a gate, and then a steep downhill to reach another gate, and into a field with livestock. Walk to the bottom of the livestock field and up on the other side. Then through the gate, cross the road and you will reach the entrance to Greys Court.

Through the gate, head over to the immaculate road and follow it up.

After a little bit more uphill, you will get lovely views out to the hills on the right and some of the buildings of Greys Court to the left.

FUN FACT:

If you decide to enter Greys Court, you'll see gardens which have been around since the 13th century. Also, 13 women have owned or co-owned Greys Court.

You can have a little exploration here, but to continue with the walk, stay on the road to reach the car park, then walk through it keeping to the left. This will lead you to an opening with the trail.

Leave the car park along this trail, and continue down the hill then up through a gate to reach the woods on the left. You will be walking straight for a while now, but taking gates on the left.

Go through the gate on the left, but stay walking in the same direction.

At the next lot of gates, go through the left one but stay in this direction still. You will get a lovely view of a house across the field soon, and then you will reach the road.

Possible detour

Now, if you'd like to see some really impressive trees, you can do a little detour here. You will have to walk back to this road after though.

Option 1. To continue with the walk, you turn right on this road to walk towards the house, which you will see at the end.

Option 2. For the detour, cross the road and go into the woods ahead on the right. In the woods it will feel like the lights have been turned off. In all the woods I have walked in my life, I've never seen anything like this. It's a little scary, but it doesn't go on too long before you are walking through nice lighter woods alongside the road. Keep going and the trees get bigger, and more impressive. I only discovered this because I walked this way by accident once. It was also autumn at the time, and everything was so bright and orange. I felt like I was in an orange autumn wonderland.

Continue on with the walk

Now, if you took the detour, walk back to the road then towards the house. Just before you reach it there is a trail on the left, but don't worry if you miss it, as when you reach the house, you can just turn left there.

Then go through the gate heading towards the woods. The gate says private but it's ok for walkers.

Navigate through Lambridge Wood

This next chunk of walk is that vast and confusing woodland. As you go deeper, two things happen. Lots of trails start to appear here and there, and the trail you are on sometimes feels like it disappears.

Luckily there are now those white arrows on the trees to guide you through. You are going to keep following the arrows, then when you reach the trail signpost, turn right, and follow the next lot of white arrows.

At this point there should be a field past the woods to the right. As long as you keep that just there to your right, you are going the correct way.

Keep following this trail, which will then curve to the right, and take you down a hill then back up again.

When you reach a junction where the right trail leads to a gate, take that one. Through the gate you will be in the Badgemore Golf Course.

The golf course

It's not a proper English countryside walk without a golf course.

There is no trail here. You just need to walk straight. Stay straight and trust that you are doing it right, and you will eventually reach the path.

This will lead you alongside a fence and field to the left, which has llamas (or alpacas...one of them).

When you reach a gate on the left, go through it and continue along the drive.

Walk back to Henley

The drive leads to residential road, and at the road bend, there is a left trail taking you behind one of the houses. This feels a little like a back alley, countryside style.

This will lead you downhill to the next residential road. This final bit of the walk isn't very interesting, as it's all residential. But it doesn't go on for too long. Turn right on this road, then take the next road on the right 'Hop Gardens'.

This will lead you back to the main road you started the walk on.

What you should do here though, is take the road on the left just before the main road. You will know what I mean when you are there.

This will lead you back into town past some nice, old but quaint buildings to finish.

PUBLIC TRANSPORT

You can reach the High Weald a few ways by train, some will take you right into it, some on the edge. The walks in this guide use the following trains with a journey time ranging from 40 min to 1h45min from London.

London Bridge – Thameslink, Southeastern

London St Pancras – Thameslink, Southeastern

London Blackfriars – Thameslink

London Charing Cross – Southeastern

London Victoria – Southern

WALK 17
Ouse Valley Viaduct and the Ardingly Reservoir
8 miles

WALK 18
Etchingham to Robertsbridge via Bodiam Castle
11.5 miles

WALK 19
Hastings to Rye
12.5 miles

WALK 20
Tunbridge Wells to Eridge Rocks
14 miles

WALK 21
The Forest Way: East Grinstead to Groombridge
11 miles

HIGH WEALD NATIONAL LANDSCAPE

High Weald is very old, with its key features being established by the 14th century, and it's said to be one of the best surviving coherent medieval landscapes in Northern Europe. Here you will find a few castles, historic farmsteads, and ancient woodland. About one third of the High Weald is woodland. You'll also find lots of fields and meadows, and maybe some bog.

I find walking here feels very farmy, and wild, with a definite old world feeling to it, and with some of the muddiest areas I have walked near London.

Located south of London, nestled between the South Downs and the Surrey Hills and Kent Downs, the High Weald covers 908 square miles across Surrey, Sussex and Kent. This one was designated an AONB (now National Landscape) in 1983.

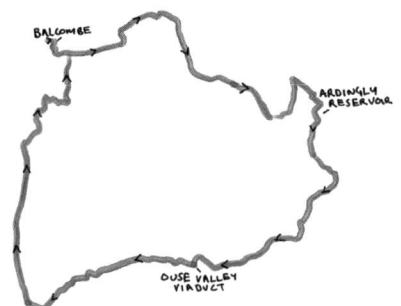

WALK 17

Ouse Valley Viaduct and the Ardingly Reservoir

This is a lovely walk taking you to the famous Ouse Valley Viaduct, and then around the tranquil Ardingly Reservoir, with a bit of a countryside stomp in between.

The Ouse Valley Viaduct is basically a very ornate railway bridge, built in the 1840's to connect London to Brighton, it has 37 arches, and is Grade II listed.

I had always done this walk in the opposite direction, but then one day realised that if I walked the other way, I could finish at a pub, which sounded much more sensible.

It turned out that I prefer this way around, as I would say that the walk can be split into two distinct sections. 'Before reservoir', and 'reservoir'. 'Before reservoir' is much more rugged, and then 'reservoir' is gentle and easy. It's better to get the rugged out of the way first.

After that it's just a short walk back to Balcombe, and maybe another hill.

WHAT TO EXPECT

Out of the station you get onto the trail pretty quick. Alongside a road at first and then it's the field, woods, and fields again, with a bit of an uphill. You'll reach the highest point in the walk before heading back down, with wonderful views all around and the viaduct below.

There's then a few more fields, a bit of road, and potentially lots of mud. You'll get a good view of the viaduct before arriving, which peaks the excitement. When you get there, you can go and stand by it for that famous shot (you might have to wait your turn as it's quite a popular one).

FUN FACT:

The viaduct is said to be made up of over 11 million bricks, some from the Netherlands (although this hasn't been officially confirmed).

It's then a few more fields, and maybe a hill, to reach the Ardingly Reservoir. From there it's a nice easy, and only slightly rugged trail, to take you around it.

After that it's just a short walk back to Balcombe, and maybe another hill, where you can finish at the pub before heading to the station.

Ouse Valley Viaduct and the Ardingly Reservoir

DIRECTORY

LOGISTICS:

Start/Finish: Balcombe Station, Sussex.
Difficulty: Easy/moderate.
Type: Circular.
Route Distance: 8 miles/13 km.
Time: 3h 20min.

HOW TO GET THERE:

Direct trains from London Bridge, journey time 40 min on weekdays (a bit longer on weekends). You can also catch that same train from London St Pancras or Blackfriars.

COMING BY CAR:

You can park at the Ardingly Reservoir RH17 6SQ. You can follow the same walk route, or freestyle and walk over to the viaduct (1 mile), then back and partway around the reservoir, then back (there isn't a circular trail around the reservoir).

ELEVATION GAIN:

409m/1342ft.

TERRAIN:

Grassy fields, dirt tracks, some mud, a bit of road, stiles.

DOG FRIENDLY:

Yes, with some restrictions. The stiles have doggy sized holes. Some fields they will need to be on a lead. Can be loose livestock about.

PHONE SIGNAL:

Yes until the viaduct. Parts with no signal around the reservoir.

PUBLIC TOILETS:

Yes, at the station, and at the reservoir activity centre (only during opening hours).

IDEAL TIME OF YEAR:

Can get muddy after rain. Otherwise, any time is good.

OPTION TO SHORTEN THE WALK:

Yes, but you will have to miss out the reservoir. From the station, walk to the viaduct then turn back. This will be about 6 miles.

WHERE TO EAT?

Only a few options on this walk.

CAFE AND COFFEE:

Balcombe

- The Balcombe Tea Rooms (dogs not allowed inside).
- Fabs Fabulous Pizza (takeaway food truck).

On the walk

- The Ardingly Activity Centre Cafe (seasonal opening hours/ dog friendly).

PUB:

Balcome

- The Half Moon Inn (dog friendly).

FOR SUPPLIES:
Balcombe Stores.

TIPS/OTHER THINGS TO KNOW

- The reservoir is being restored, with no completion date set. If it's not completed when you do the walk, some parts will be under scaffolding, but it doesn't affect the walk.
- Lots of mud after rain. The kind that sucks your whole foot in. I'd recommend wearing gaiters.
- In all weather I recommend hiking boots.
- There are a lot of benches around the reservoir for a break, and lots of bins. There is usually a lack of bins along walks. Not on this one.
- If you want to add a bit extra to the walk, you can rent water sports equipment from the Ardingly Activity Centre. It's by the car park.
- It will likely be busy around the viaduct area on summer weekends. On the section before the viaduct I've rarely passed anyone.
- Balcombe Station is a bit more out on the edge of town, so if you do the walk in the other direction, you will have to go past the station to head into town to reach the pub, which is why that way around is less efficient.

> *Don't worry, it's a quiet road, and actually quite pretty with the trees.*

ROUTE DESCRIPTION

You need to exit the station from platform 1. If you have arrived from London direction, you will arrive on platform 2.

Out of the station turn left through the car park, and take the trail on the right just before the main road. This will take you under the trees, where you turn left to walk parallel to the road.

When you reach the road again, a short way along you'll see a trail signpost pointing right. Follow it.

After a bit less than 1/2 a mile (from the station) you will reach a crop field, where you turn right to walk around the perimeter.

On the other side, there will be a gap to the right with a wooden bridge. Go that way.

You will now enter more woods, and a short way along follow the trail as it curves to the right. It's a bit of a hill here, then when you reach an opening with multiple turns, continue to the very top, and turn left along the top to continue up the hill.

This will lead you out of the woods, and into the fields, where you will have some wonderful views, and might be able to see the viaduct nestled behind some trees below.

Walk to the viaduct

You now need to continue walking in a straight direction, down the hill to reach the stile at the bottom.

In the next mini field, walk straight across and through a gate, and then keep going down the hill. The trail is quite obvious here, and there are trail arrows to guide you. At the bottom you will reach a road, and potentially a big patch of bog and mud.

Turn left on the road, and a few meters along turn right to get back onto the trail in a field.

Walk along the right perimeter of the field, which will lead you to a road on the other end (and a bit more mud). At the road turn right.

Don't worry, it's a quiet road, and actually quite pretty with the trees. It is uphill though.

Continue up it and then down the other side to reach a main road. On the other side of the road to the left is a drive to the Great Bentley Farm. Follow that.

Go through the gate to the farm, and continue on this driveway road for about 1/2 a mile, then just before the houses, look out for a trail sign and gate in the bushes to the left. Through the gate, walk along the right side of the field, then stay on the edge as it curves to the right, then a short way after, cut across the field to the left to reach a wooden bridge.

Over the bridge you want to walk in a diagonal right, about 2 o'clock, which will lead you to an opening to get into another field. It will also lead you to possibly the muddiest, boggiest section of the walk.

In the next field, continue in the same direction, cutting diagonally across the field, to reach a series of two gates. This will lead you onto an enclosed trail to the left.

A short way after you will reach the sheds and cottage. Continue past them, then a bit after the road takes you left, you should see a big footpath sign ahead, pointing right into a field. When you enter this field you will suddenly be presented with the Ouse Valley Viaduct ahead.

Now head diagonally across the field towards it.

When you get there, you can walk under it some way. Which way depends on what part is under scaffolding, or if it's completed. It will be easy to figure out when you are there.

Now have some fun taking photos.

Walk to Ardingly Reservoir

On the other side of the viaduct, walk across the field to reach the road, where you turn right.

Continue over the bridge, where there will be a trail into a field on the left just after. Continue straight along the edge of the field, all the way to the other end, where you will be led onto a wide dirt path.

When you reach the next field, follow the obvious trail as it curves ahead to the left to reach a wooden bridge. Over the bridge, take the trail on a diagonal right which then curves to the left around the trees, which will lead you to another wooden bridge, which strangely you need to climb over.

Now continue up the hill, keeping to the right edge, then partway up (about 160m), look out for an opening in the bushes on the right, and walk through it. In the next field, continue walking along the right edge which will lead you to a gate. Through the gate, stay on this main path and a short way along you will reach the reservoir.

Walk around the Ardingly Reservoir

You should see the trail around the reservoir straight ahead, with the activity centre on the left. If you get onto the trail, this will take you around the right side of the reservoir. It's now as simple as following this trail.

It's a nice trail, easy to follow, but can get a little more rugged and very muddy in parts. Surrounded by trees, it's very peaceful.

After about 1 mile you will reach a road. Follow it to the left and then back along the other side of the reservoir. It's another mile or so along this side of the reservoir to reach the road. Just a warning, this side is a bit more rugged and muddy.

At the road, turn left, to walk down and then over the bridge towards some cottages. Very enviable cottages. These people get to have the reservoir as part of their front lawns.

Past the cottage with the pastel door you should see some steps on the left. Go up them.

Walk to Balcombe

Up the steps, you will reach a field. There are now two ways back from here.

Option 1: Take the trail straight up along the edge of the field. This will lead you to the main road, where you turn right. It's then about 1/2 a mile to reach the town centre.

Option 2: This way keeps you in fields and nature to reach Balcombe, however, there is one short bit of country road, with a blind bend, and no walkway. It's a bit more dangerous, so if you do it, you need to be very careful. This is the way I will describe…

So, once up the steps, continue to the junction, and turn right. This will take you under the trees, then just ahead at the junction, turn to the left, and follow this all the way to the road (the one you need to be careful on).

At the road, turn left, to walk around the corner, then a short way along there will be a gap in the hedge on the right. You won't be able to see it until you are right next to it. You will be on this road for about 150m.

Through the gap is a stile to get you into a field. The danger is over. Now continue straight across the field to the other side, and over a wooden bridge. Then continue straight up along the edge of the next field to reach a gate at the top on the left.

There are some wonderful views as you make your way up there.

Go through this gate, and along the wide dirt trail lined with trees to reach the field. In the field turn right. You should see some houses ahead, and a line of bushes leading to them. That's the trail. So follow the edge of this field to reach it, and up to the houses.

You are now in Balcombe.

When you reach the road, follow it, as it curves to the left, and you will be led right to the village store and the pub just next to it.

After you've enjoyed the pub, it's a bit under 1/2 a mile to reach the station from here.

WALK 18

Etchingham to Robertsbridge via Bodiam Castle

This walk takes you through the Rother Valley, ancient woods, and farms, with a few oast houses along the way (those ones with pointy roofs), an impressive 14th century moated castle, before finishing off in a very quaint historic village with medieval houses.

There are some really wonderful views on this one, but there is also a fair bit of road. I don't find the road too bad, and for me, the rest of the walk makes up for it.

It is also one of the muddiest, boggiest walks I have done in England, actually, the New Forest might be worse, but this is a close second. If there has been recent heavy rain, about 2/3 of the walk will be mud and bog… probably the reason why I don't mind the road.

*A village dating back to the
11th century.
And it looks like it.*

WHAT TO EXPECT

It's about 8 miles to reach the castle, and this is also my favourite stretch of the walk. All the good stuff is here. First it's some fields and meadows, then it's the ancient woods, which are very rugged and wild, with getting lost potential. If walking through straggly woods with barely visible trails makes you a bit nervous, you might not want to do this one alone. Then it's some more meadows, farms, lovely views, and a few oast house sightings, to reach Bodiam Castle. This section of the walk is the hilly part.

There is a nice path you can follow all around the castle with some benches.

The remainder of the walk to reach Robertsbridge I don't find as interesting as the rest, but it's decent enough. It's not so hilly, so that's good. It's a sort of ridge walk at first, alongside the River Rother. Then there is a pretty nasty road section with fast cars and no pavement. Luckily it's not for too long, before some more fields and meadows, before finishing with road. This road is fine. Very peaceful, and some nice cottages, and more oast houses before reaching Robertsbridge which is the nice surprise ending. A village dating back to the 11th century. And it looks like it.

FUN FACT:

Gray-Nicolls cricket bats (an iconic cricket bat brand) has its origins in Robertsbridge. Nicolls was an independent cricket bat maker in Robertsbridge, before joining forces with Gray who also made bats in Cambridge.

DIRECTORY

LOGISTICS:

Start/Finish: Etchingham Station, Robertsbridge Station. East Sussex.
Difficulty: Moderate.
Type: Point to point.
Route Distance: 11.5 miles/18.5 km.
Time: 4–5h.

HOW TO GET THERE:

Direct trains from London Bridge (or Charing Cross) on Southeastern. Buy a return ticket to Robertsbridge and get off one stop early in Etchingham. Journey time: 1h10–1h30min, dependending on which train.

COMING BY CAR:

The only car park is at Bodiam Castle which is National Trust.

ELEVATION GAIN:

330m/1083ft.

TERRAIN:

Mud, bog, grass, dirt, road, bridges, lots of stiles.

DOG FRIENDLY:

Not the most, depends on the size of your dog. Most of the stiles don't have doggy holes. Would need to be on a lead through some fields. Not allowed inside Bodiam Castle, but allowed outside.

PHONE SIGNAL:

Patchy throughout the whole walk.

PUBLIC TOILETS:

At Bodiam Castle or Robertsbridge.

IDEAL TIME OF YEAR:

Summer is best, due to the bog and mud.

OPTION TO SHORTEN THE WALK:

Maybe. There is a bus near Bodiam Castle, but it takes you to Hastings. Another option is to start from Robertsbridge and walk to the castle and back which will be 8 miles. But you will miss out the best section of the walk.

WHERE TO EAT?
CAFE AND COFFEE:

Bodiam

• Cafe at the National Trust Centre (dog friendly).

Robertsbridge

• Judges Bakery (dogs not allowed inside).

PUB:

Bodiam

• The Castle Inn by Bodiam Castle (dog friendly)

Robertsbridge

• The George Inn (former 18th century coaching inn/ dog friendly).

FOR SUPPLIES:

A convenience store in Robertsbridge.

TIPS/OTHER THINGS TO KNOW

- If you do want to do this in wetter months, I highly recommend using gaiters. It can get impossibly wet and boggy. I would completely avoid after long stretches of heavy rain as it can also get flooded.
- Hiking boots are recommended any time.
- You don't need to pay to walk around Bodiam Castle. If you do decide you want to go inside, you can buy tickets out the other end from where you enter.

> *This is ancient woods, and it's a bit confusing here, with strong getting lost possibility.*

ROUTE DESCRIPTION

Out of the station from platform 2, head through the car park and turn left on the main road. After the second bridge, look out for a stile onto the field on the left, then follow the trail across it. The trail is at your 1 o'clock, and takes you around the left side of the field, to a bridge on the other side.

Over the bridge turn right to walk alongside the river, with an electric fence to your left. It's quite close. This trail will lead you over a wooden bridge, then continue straight across the next (potentially boggy) field to the gate on the other side.

You will be at a road now, with a gate opposite. Go through the gate. This will lead you to another gate, which you go through and turn left.

A short way along, when you reach the grass trail split, take the left one and continue on this grass trail through the meadow for a bit. When you walk through the bushes, straight ahead across the next meadow you should see a wooden bridge on the other side. Head to that.

Across the bridge, continue along a dirt trail now, up a bit of a hill, then over the stile onto the track, where you turn left. Follow this track, then over another stile, and on the right you should see a farm shelter.

Turn to the right here, then past the shelter, over another stile. This trail will lead you downhill and into Burgh Wood.

Navigate through Burgh Wood

This is ancient woods, and it's a bit confusing here, with strong getting lost possibility. I will direct you as best I can. You are going to be walking in a straight-ish direction, with some little curves here and there. Although it will feel like you are deep in some wild remote forest, it's not actually that big, so if you get lost, don't panic.

I've actually only done this walk in wet months. Don't ask me why. When the ground is covered in leaves, with ankle deep mud. So it could be that during summer, the trail is obvious.

When you enter the woods, stay on the main trail. After the more open bit, you should pass a gas high pressure pipeline to your right. A little unnerving.

At the next slightly more open area, stay straight, and you should reach a wooden bridge. Over the bridge, continue straight up the hill, then when you hit a tree dead end, head over to your diagonal left, and you should reach a trail, where you turn right to continue up the hill.

When you reach a main junction, turn left, and stay on this trail now all the way to the end, where you turn left again.

When you reach a trail split, take the right one. You should be able to see a dog poo bin at the end. Like the light at the end of a tunnel.

When you reach the poo bin, don't exit the woods, but turn to the left to continue walking along the edge of them. This will lead you out the other end, into a residential area. Stay straight through here to reach the main road, where you turn right. This is Hurst Green.

Walk through the farms

Walk along the road (with pavement, don't panic), and turn left just after the building with a clock tower.

You will now be on a dirt road, which will lead you to Driftways Farm. Continue along the road through the farm, and it will lead you onto a dirt and grass track. Now follow this alongside the fields, then after the open area, pick it up again on the other side, and keep following it all the way towards some woods to the right.

When you reach the trees, go through them, then up a small hill, and turn left so the trees and bushes are on your right. There should be trail signs guiding you.

Continue to the end of the meadow then through some more trees to reach a large field. In the field, now walk around the left edge. When you reach the other end, turn left, then after some more trees when you reach the next field, keep to the left still. You will be walking along the bottom of a hill, with woodland up it to your right.

When you reach the junction, turn left, and follow this trail all the way to the road. At the road, turn right, then just ahead at the main road, go across it to continue on the road opposite, up the hill.

You have about 1/2 a mile on this road now. It is a country road, but I've not found it to be that busy, and it's fairly wide (I've been on much worse). If you are tall, you can see over the hedge for some nice views across the fields and hills, with little houses nestled in the trees.

Keep going until you reach Conghurst Farm on the right, then enter. A short way along there is a fork, stay on the right to walk past an oast house and other farm buildings. Stay on this road through to reach the fields, then continue on the track on the left.

Some wonderful views here.

Follow this track down the hill, then near the bottom, you want to turn right. There is an obvious trail here. Make sure you are on the right side of the hedge. (Note. It's the second turning you will pass, the first one with a big tree isn't a public right of way). Now follow this to the other side of the field, then when the hedge ends and there is a crop field in front, walk along the right side of it, and you should reach a wooden bridge.

Over the bridge, you will walk through some trees and bushes, then along the right side of a field. Near the other end of the field you will reach a trail sign. Turn left here to cut across the field along the trail.

There's more wonderful views along here across the rolling hills.

Keep following this trail and it will lead you up to some horse stables. When you get there, turn left.

At the next big junction, take the right. This will take you along a grass trail, then dirt trail, through a small bit of woods, over a stream and stile, then uphill along more grass lined with hedges. When you reach a junction, stay straight to head into another farm, but when the track curves to the left to the farm buildings, you should see a gate straight ahead leading to the cottages. Take that.

Nearly there now.

Walk to Bodiam Castle

You now have about 1/2 a mile along the road again, but this is only for people who live here so it's not heavily trafficked. I quite like it, passing by the cottages and farm. It's also a nice break from the mud and bog.

When you reach the main road, turn right, then a few meters along, turn left on the right side of the house.

You will enter a big crop field. You now need to walk diagonally through the middle of it, uphill, towards a big tree on the other end.

As you make your way up, make sure to look back for a nice view to an oast house.

At the top, past the tree, the trail will lead you to the left.

After you pass through a gate, you will be in a small hill field. Partway through, instead of walking straight up the hill, turn to the right to walk up it. This will lead you to a stile, and road.

Cross straight over the road and up the mini hill. Stay walking in this same direction, crossing over the path again, and you should reach a trail sign next to a hedge.

Follow the trail to the right, with the hedge to your left.

This will then take you downhill, where you should get a view to Bodiam Castle through the trees on your right. Keep going all the way, to reach a stile to get you into the Bodiam Castle ground.

And you are there.

You can have a walk all the way around, and there are a few benches about to sit and admire the castle. It's quite spectacular from the outside. The inside is ruins, with a tower, spiral staircases, and a portcullis (a latticed medieval gate), which is apparently quite rare now. Walking inside you can imagine the knights that once roamed here.

Walk to Robertsbridge

After you are done with castle stuff, it's time to head to Robertsbridge. It's about 4 miles from here.

You now want to make your way to the main road. One way to do it is to walk to the other side of the castle, to the right corner from where you entered is a trail, which leads to the car park and National Trust centre and cafe.

When you get there, turn right and you will reach the road. The Castle Inn pub is just opposite if you want to pop in.

At the road, turn left. A short way along, you will reach the bridge over the River Rother. The trail will be on the right just before the bridge. You won't see it until you are right on it.

Take this trail, and you now follow a ridge with the river to your left. You can walk on top of the ridge, which might be wise if there is some flooding.

When you reach the ridge junction, stay straight. You are now going to follow this for a bit over 1 mile to reach the road. At the road, turn left. As you make your way alongside the road, look out for the steam railway tracks to the left.

It then gets a bit nasty. The trail disappears and you have to walk on the road for a bit, which has fast cars. Don't worry, it's not for too long. After maybe 100m or so, you should see a

Etchingham to Robertsbridge via Bodiam Castle

trail sign and a gap in the hedges on the right. Go through it.

If there is a sign there saying the trail ahead is closed, don't worry, that doesn't affect this walk.

Now continue along the edge of the field, with the river to your left, and when you see a concrete bridge on the left, go over it, then turn right to now walk with the river to your right. Follow this now all the way to the trees (and keep an eye out for a pillbox on the other side of the river).

When you reach the trees and the next field, continue along the left edge of it.

It could be very boggy in here. Just a warning.

Walk to the other end, and then turn right, continuing along the edge of the field. Then at the next corner, turn left to enter another field. There should be a trail sign here.

Now continue straight, walking along the right side of this field. This will lead you to a dirt trail further along with a big mass of water to the left. When I first saw it, I had a moment of panic thinking that I would have to wade through it, luckily you don't have to. I must say though, I don't trust that the mass of water won't overflow and flood everything. I've not seen it do that, but it looks like it could.

The trail will lead you to a stile, then once over, continue straight across the field towards the houses on the other side. When you reach the houses, continue on the road ahead to the right. You will now be on this road the rest of the way, about 1 mile.

The first part of it I quite enjoy. Apart from being dry, you will pass some cottages, a couple of oast houses, and lots of trees. Then towards the end it gets a little boring.

Just before you reach the main road (the A21), you should see a wide trail leading uphill to the left. Follow that and it will lead you to the bridge over the road. On the other side you will be in Robertsbridge.

I didn't know anything about the place when first I arrived and was pleasantly surprised with all the old timber framed buildings, which I now know some of the oldest surviving ones date back as far as the 14th century.

Now, continue straight along the residential street, and it will lead you to the high street. When you get there, turn left.

To get to the pub, stay straight along here. To get to the station, take the first right.

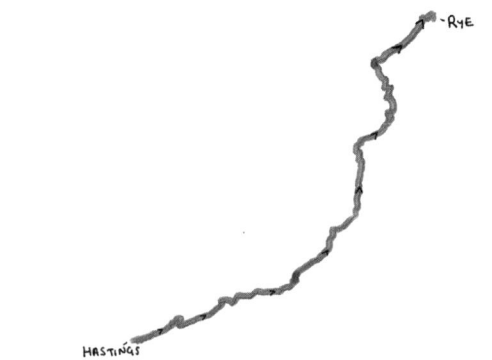

WALK 19

Hastings to Rye

This walk takes you between two medieval towns, with roots in the ancient Kingdom of the South Saxons. Rye with its cobblestone lanes and medieval half timbered houses. Secret passageways, tales of smugglers, home to poets and artists. Then there's Hastings Old Town, with quaint streets crisscrossed by narrow passages known as twittens. You will find cute independent cafes, boutique shops, a thriving art scene, medieval houses, some dating back to 1450. It was actually voted Britain's best walking neighbourhood in 2018.

The two towns are linked by a walking route called the Saxons Shore Way. The route I have devised actually takes a slightly different route. But feel free to follow the full Saxon Shore Way. It will take you via Camber Castle.

Overall, it's a fantastic walk, and in parts reminds me of the South West Coast path. Very hilly. Lots of nature, and a feeling like you are miles from civilisation.

If you do the walk in spring you might see lots of lambs. I once came across a sheep that had literally just given birth to two lambs. They still had 'birth stuff' on them.

Dense fairytale woodland, with lots of hills and steps.

WHAT TO EXPECT

You have a big hill right at the start, with a fantastic view looking over Hastings, and to the castle in the distance. Then it's a bit of field and dirt trails to reach the woods. Dense fairytale woodland, with lots of hills and steps.

There is the occasional cliff view, but not that much compared to other coastal walks.

There is then a brief walk through the village of Fairlight, and after 7 miles you descend off the cliffs to Pett Level, with the option for a dip in the sea. You can actually stay on the coast and follow it all the way to Rye via Rye Harbour, but I prefer this way.

The walk now turns inland along the Royal Military Canal. It's nice and flat, then there's one more hill into the village of Winchelsea, before finishing at Rye. There are two route options to get to Rye. One is across the meadows, and another is a bit of road, but you do pass a very 'interesting' road sign name, and then a nice dirt trail to the end.

FUN FACT:

There is a road called Dumb Woman's Lane. I've heard a number of theories about it. This area was once a smuggling route, and one theory is that a woman who witnessed the smugglers had her tongue cut off so she couldn't tell anyone. Another is that the woman played dumb so as not to give away the location of the men of the village.

DIRECTORY

LOGISTICS:

Start/Finish: Hastings Station, Rye Station. East Sussex.
Difficulty: Challenging.
Type: Point to point.
Route Distance: 12.5 miles/20 km.
Time: 4h.

HOW TO GET THERE:

Buy a return ticket from London St Pancras to Hastings. Part of the journey will be on the Southeastern High Speed train, and part on Southern, with a change at Ashford International. This will then cover your return journey from Rye. Outward journey 1.5h, return about 1h. *There is a direct train to Hastings from London Bridge, but you won't be able to return from Rye with this ticket.*

COMING BY CAR:

A number of car parks in Hastings. An option is Pelham Place car park TN34 3AD. You can then get a train from Rye back to Hastings at the end. Journey time: 22min. Or park in Rye at Lucknow Place car park TN31 7LR, then get a train to Hastings to start the walk. Both are RingGo app payments.

ELEVATION GAIN:

524m/1719ft.

TERRAIN:

Hills, steps, dirt trail, grass, and some road.

DOG FRIENDLY:

Yes. Apart from Pett Level beach, not allowed during the summer months (1 May to 30 Sept). You don't need to go onto the beach for this walk though.

PHONE SIGNAL:

Patchy. Poor signal in the woods. Ok everywhere else.

PUBLIC TOILETS:

Yes. At Hastings Station, and in the car park at Rye Station. Also in the car parks if coming by car.

IDEAL TIME OF YEAR:

Any time is good. After rain it will be a bit muddy though.

OPTION TO SHORTEN THE WALK:

Yes. At 11 miles you can catch a train from Winchelsea Station, this will get you to Rye or Hastings, or back up towards London.

WHERE TO EAT?

Lots of options at the start, during, and end of the walk. Rye is also quite posh which is reflected in the food. Here are some suggestions.

CAFE AND COFFEE:

Hastings
- Hanushka Coffee House (dog friendly).
- The Famous Cod Father fish bar in Hastings (dogs allowed outside).

On the walk
- 7 miles: Eaters@Pett (a little hut style cafe by the beach at Pett Level/ dog friendly).

Rye
- Whitehouse Rye (dog friendly).
- The Cobbles Tea Room in Rye (dog friendly).
- Mermaid Street Cafe (for less posh/ dog friendly).

PUB:

Hastings
- Ye Olde Pumphouse (dog friendly).

On the walk
- 5 miles: The Cove Pub, in Fairlight Cove (dog friendly).
- 11 miles: The New Inn, in Winchelsea (dog friendly).

Rye
- Old Bell Rye (dog friendly).

FOR SUPPLIES:

Multiple supermarkets in Hastings. In Rye is Jempson's Supermarket, and The Rye Deli which has excellent salad boxes.

TIPS/OTHER THINGS TO KNOW

- Spend some time in Rye at the end. It's a very charming historic town, with Tudor buildings and the famous Mermaid Street.
- Remember to take swimwear/towel if you fancy a dip in the sea at Pett Level (or the secret beach. I'll explain a bit later).
- If you're considering walking in the other direction, don't. This way is better. Get the hills out of the way first, and Rye is a wonderful place to finish.
- Hiking boots recommended.

*I knew if I headed towards the moo,
I would get to an open field where I could then
use the sun and wind for navigation.*

ROUTE DESCRIPTION

From Hastings Station, head towards East Hill. For easiest navigation just head to the seafront and turn left. Make sure to walk on the left side of the road when you get there. After a short walk, passing by some seaside amusement stuff, you will reach a side road forking off this one to the left. Take it. This will lead you through the charming Hastings Old Town.

It's a good place to grab a coffee and prepare for the hill.

East Hill

Continue along to the end of the street, and you will see the Blue Dolphin Fish Bar straight ahead. It's bright blue. Walk along the right side of it, and you should get a view across to a big hill ahead. That's the one you are heading to.

Keep going, across another road, towards these big black sheds. On the left, next to the Dolphin Inn, is a narrow passage with steps. Go up them.

Up the steps, follow the signs for East Hill to the right and up more steps. At the road, just across it to the left are more steps. Keep going up. There's some great views across the rooftops of Hastings as you make your way up. A good excuse to take some breaks.

You'll reach a sign saying 'Hastings Country Park Nature Reserve East Hill'. To the right are some steps. Take those. Just keep going up steps until there are no more, and you will reach a large open green space. From here you can enjoy more views over Hastings.

Walk across the green now, keeping right. You will be led through some bushes, and around the corner will have a nice view to the cliffs ahead. Keep to the right, following the coast path signs, past more bushes, to reach the woods.

The woods

In the woods, turn right. Going forwards, at any junction, keep to the right, following the signs for the coast path.

The first time I came here, the right was closed. So I went straight and found myself in a maze of fairytale woodland. I got so lost I didn't know which way was up. I accidentally closed down my online map, and had no phone signal, so couldn't get it back. This was a first, getting lost on a coastal walk. I could hear a cow mooing in the distance. I knew if I headed towards the moo I would get to an open field where I could then use the sun and wind for navigation… or my phone signal would return. So be sure to turn right.

This will take you downhill, under tree cover, then out to the open in a dip in the cliffs. It's quite spectacular when you arrive, in the cliff dip surrounded by greenery. You do have some steps though, first down, then back up the other side.

As you make your way up the other side, make sure to look back for a wonderful cliff view.

The open

You'll reach a flatter green area, with a fenced off field in the middle. Turn left here. You can take either left, as they both join up later on. Just a note, the second left can get very muddy in winter.

When you reach a trail split, either is fine, then take a right at the next junction.

Walk to Fairlight Cove

You will be in the woods again, and soon there are more steps. Down, then up. And hills too, down, then up. And more steps, down then up. It's very hilly. Going between woods and open, and woods again. Oh, and remember to take the right at any junctions.

If you fancy a little extra surprise, somewhere along this stretch you will notice a big sign saying 'beach closed, enter at your own risk'. If you decide to enter at your own risk you will reach a hidden beach where people go to sunbathe without any clothes on. It's pretty rugged getting there, and involves using a rope to help get down, but you will be rewarded with a little paradise at the end.

Sticking with the main path, after just under 4 miles, the worst of the hills are over, and you will now be fully out in the open with wonderful views ahead, and back.

There is an interesting trail split coming up. You know how I say to always keep to the right trail following the coast path signs. Well, for some reason the coast path sign here tells you to take the left. You can, as they both join up ahead, but I like to take the right still.

This will lead you to the village of Fairlight Cove. There isn't much here, just houses and one place to eat. It's about a 10min walk through to get back onto the trail. It's well signposted, but here is the route in case any signs are missing…

Take the second left onto Shepherds Way, then the first right onto Bramble Way. Further ahead, the road will curve to the left, then take the first right which will lead you onto a narrow alley type trail.

At the end, turn left onto the road, then at the next end, turn right. Keep going right to the end where the road bends right. Don't bend with it. The trail is straight ahead through the bushes at the bend. Take that.

Pett Level

Through the bushes, turn right, and follow the trail around the fenced field. It will get quite narrow in parts. You will soon reach a large open green space (and a bit of a hill, but not like the others, so don't panic). There is a great view looking back from here.

There are a few more steps to reach another green space with a nice bench to sit on, and some more cliffy views.

The trail will then lead you through some trees and bushes, to reach a nice viewpoint to Pett Level beach below. You are now going to descend towards it, along a narrow trail, with bushes to the right and fence and cottages to the left. One of them has a thatched roof, which is nice. When you reach the road at the bottom, turn right.

A short way along, the Royal Military Canal will be to the left. If you want to visit the beach, turn to the right here. For this walk though, you follow the canal. So when you are done with the beach, come back here.

Walk to Winchelsea

Now follow the canal. At first on the left side of it, then cross over the little bridge to walk along the right side of it.

You will be guided along a dirt and grass trail, with fields with cows and sheep to the right, the canal to your left and a hill ahead. Yes, I'm sorry, it's another hill. Oh, and look out for a pillbox on the left.

When you reach a bridge, cross the canal, then a few meters ahead, there is an almost hidden little bridge on the right. Go over that too.

Now walk to the left, and follow the trail which then leads towards the hill.

When you get to it, the easiest way up is a bit to the right, where there should be a trail sign. As you make your way up, you will reach some foot holes to the left to help you up.

At the gate, go through, and follow the perimeter of the field along the right edge.

It's a bit more uphill now, then at the top, turn right through the gate, and follow this trail across the field to the next gate. There is a nice view back to the sea up here.

Through the gate, you will be on the road. Turn right, then there is a gate a few meters along to the left. Go through it and turn right and now head across the field towards the farm cottages you will see ahead.

Past the cottages, cross over a mini road and through another gate to the next field, and keep going straight across it. Through the next gate, follow the trail to the left and then up the hill to reach a black gate. Through here you have two options. You can follow the trail to the left which will lead you to the road. Or go over the stile into Chapel Field.

If you take the Chapel Field route, continue left up the hill towards a wall ruin to reach the road. There is a stone type stile to get onto the road. At the road, turn right, and it will lead you into Winchelsea. You will walk past the church, and a pub if you fancy a break.

Walk to Rye

At the end of the road, turn left. This will lead you through an archway ruin.

The next bit isn't so fun. You will be on the main road which is quite busy. There is a strip of pavement you can walk on though. Continue down the hill, and at the hairpin bend in the road take the road that leads off it ahead to the right.

Although you have to cross over at the hairpin bend, it's not scary at all. You have a good view in both directions of any oncoming traffic. You will now be on more of a residential street, and away from the main cars.

When you reach the bridge, you have two options to get to Rye.

Option 1: Just over the bridge is a trail on the right. It's the more direct route, and takes you across farm fields and meadows. It can get quite muddy though, and if it's windy it will be tough. It's easy to follow, and you basically just walk in a straight line to reach Rye.

Option 2: This way involves another mile of road unfortunately, but then you reach a really lovely trail for the rest of the way to Rye. I'll direct you this way as there is more navigation involved. If you want to go to Winchelsea Station, go this way.

So, stay following the road, which by the way, isn't too car heavy. Pass over Winchelsea Station, and keep going right to the end of the road where you will see the road sign saying 'Dumb Woman's Lane'. I was quite shocked when I saw this sign, before I knew there was a history behind it.

At Dumb Woman's Lane, turn right. Follow the road for a little, then stay straight at the bend, to join back onto the trail.

You can now follow this trail to Rye. It's a lovely trail surrounded by bushes, but also with nice views across the fields, and even a view to Camber Castle.

When you reach the road, stay following it to the right, and you will be led towards the station and town centre. Make sure to have an exploration around Rye when you arrive, and definitely visit Mermaid Street.

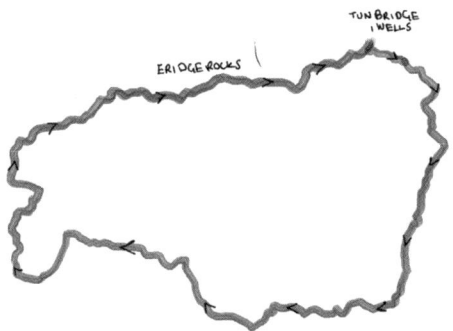

WALK 20

Tunbridge Wells to Eridge Rocks

This is a solid walk taking you from the Royal Tunbridge Wells, and on a big loop to see some very very impressive sandstone rock outcrops, passing through a lot of woods and a lot of fields along the way.

The rocks in question are Eridge Rocks, 100's of millions of years old, and a Site of Special Scientific Interest. Although, there are more. When I first set out on this walk, my target was Eridge Rocks, and I was surprised to discover that these aren't the only ones. You also have High Rocks out of Tunbridge Wells, and Harrison's Rocks in Birchden Wood. Nice little extra surprises.

Did I mention it's a woody walk?

WHAT TO EXPECT

Out of Tunbridge Wells, there is a bit of road, lots of woods, a few fields, a river, a house with a moat, and if you time it right, some steam trains, to reach Groombridge. This is the 5 mile mark, with a couple of pubs to freshen up. This first stretch is only a little bit hilly. The bigger hills come later.

After Groombridge, it's just 1 mile to reach Birchden Wood, full of huge trees, and the impressive Harrison's Rocks. You then make your way across a bit of road, and a massive crop field to reach Eridge Rocks, roughly 2 miles further along. Eridge Rocks is roughly the halfway mark (or just a little over).

It's then a little bit of road, lots more fields, some wonderful views, lots more woods, and a hill, with a chance to spot some deer, to reach the village of Frant with a nice pub.

FUN FACT:

The walk takes you past Groombridge Place which was a filming location for Pride and Prejudice.

It's not too far to Tunbridge Wells from here. Just a bit more woods (this is a very woody walk), to reach the outskirts of town.

From here it's about 2 miles to get to the station, which isn't very interesting, well, not compared to the rest of the walk anyway. It's mostly residential, with some more woods thrown in. Did I mention it's a woody walk?

DIRECTORY

LOGISTICS:

Start/Finish: Tunbridge Wells Station, Kent.
Difficulty: Moderate.
Type: Circular.
Route Distance: 14 miles/22.5 km.
Time: 5–6h.

HOW TO GET THERE:

Direct trains from London Bridge (or Charing Cross) to Tunbridge Wells on Southeastern. Journey time 45 min.

COMING BY CAR:

There is pay parking at Birchden Wood (TN3 9NH) or free parking at Eridge Rocks. In this case you could do a walk from one to the other, then back again.

ELEVATION GAIN:

472m/1549ft.

TERRAIN:

Mud, dirt trail, grass, more mud, road, some more mud, a few stiles.

DOG FRIENDLY:

Yes, but will need to be on a lead in some fields. Some loose livestock about. The stiles have doggy sized holes or gate alternatives.

PHONE SIGNAL:

Patchy. Some parts have good signal, others no signal.

PUBLIC TOILETS:

Yes. At the station, or the Birchden Wood car park.

IDEAL TIME OF YEAR:

Spring for the bluebells, or autumn for colourful leaves. I would avoid after lots of heavy rain due to the mud.

OPTION TO SHORTEN THE WALK:

Yes. From Eridge Rocks you can catch the 29 Regency Route bus back to Tunbridge Wells. This will be 8 miles. You could also just get the bus straight to the rocks from Tunbridge Wells (get off at bus stop Eridge Green Church). From there, walk along Warren Farm Lane to reach Eridge Rocks, then you can walk to Birchden Woods and back, then get the bus back. This will be 5ish miles. There is a train station in Eridge, but it's a bit of a walk off route, and on a different train line, so you would need to buy a new ticket.

WHERE TO EAT?

A few pubs along the route, then lots of options in Tunbridge Wells. Here are some suggestions.

CAFE AND COFFEE:

Tunbridge Wells

- Casa da Claudia (dog friendly).
- Juliets Cafe (dogs allowed outside).
- Fine Grind (dog friendly).

PUB:

Tunbridge Wells

- The White Bear (dog friendly).

On the walk

- 5 miles: The Junction Inn, Groomsbridge (dog friendly).
- 5 miles: Crown Inn, Groombridge (dog friendly).
- 11.5 miles: The George Inn, Frant (dog friendly).

FOR SUPPLIES:

Village store in Groombridge.
Supermarkets in Tunbridge Wells.

TIPS/OTHER THINGS TO KNOW

- I mentioned this already but I'm going to say it again to emphasise the scale of it. It is VERY MUDDY after rain.
- If you want to try something a bit different, you could combine the walk with a bit of steam train action. It runs from Tunbridge Wells to High Rocks, Groombridge, and Eridge. Tickets can be booked online or bought from the stations. Check online beforehand for timetables.

*I just did a little glance
to the left and jumped back
letting out a gasp.*

ROUTE DESCRIPTION

Out of the station turn right to walk over the bridge, then continue straight onto the high street. Keep going to the very end, then stay straight onto the next street just on the left past the Morrisons.

At the end at the church, walk to the right, then head to the green you can see across the road. It's a tricky road to cross by the way.

When you make it over there, follow the trail along the left side, then cross over the little side road onto the next green.

Follow this path past the white walled house, then when you reach the road, you should see a trail just across the other side. There is a zebra crossing just to the right to get you over there.

When you get over to that trail, follow it now through Rusthall Commons. It's nice and woody through here, and you will finally be away from the road chaos.

At the trail split, take the left, and after just under 1/2 a mile, you will reach a house. Take the trail to the left just before it. This will lead you steeply downhill.

At the bottom you will reach the road, where you turn right, then after you walk under the bridge, turn right into the housing area.

A short way in you will reach a road curve. Walk along the right which will lead you along a road with a fence to your right and houses to your left. At the end of this road, go through the gate and into the woods.

The woods

You will be walking through these woods for just under 1 mile. It can get a little confusing here. On a map there is just one trail through, but in reality there are a few trail junctions. At the first one, take the right, then at the second one take the right again. You are basically heading in a roughly straight direction, and for reference there is a railway line to your right, which you might not see at first. It will pop up a little way into the woods. There is also a hill in here.

When you reach the gate for Friezland Wood, take the main trail on the right through it. Not too far along there are these big rocks on the left. I almost didn't notice them at first. I just did a little glance to the left and jumped back letting out a gasp. I think this is High Rocks. A little taster for Eridge Rocks later.

At the end of the woods you will reach a road, where you turn left. Continue past a nice looking building on the right, which is the High Rocks wedding venue, then stay on the main road at the split ahead.

A short way further along there is a small parking area on the right. Walk into it, and the trail will be just on the other side, with a sign saying Groombridge.

Walk to Groombridge

The trail will lead you down through some straggly woods, then at the bottom, turn right to walk under the railway bridge.

This is for the steam train, which you might be able to see if you time it right.

Under the bridge, you will next go over a wooden bridge, then just continue on this main trail through the woods for about 1/2 a mile.

It can be a little spooky in here, and feels like you are somewhere that not a lot of people go. Or it could just be that I've only walked here on weekdays so everyone is at work. Maybe it is a busy trail?

When you reach a gate, continue through it straight across the edge of the field, then through another gate, and keep going straight.

You will then walk through a little more woodland, and at the end go through the big metal gate into a field. It would seem like you can't enter there, but you can. The public right of way sign is hidden. Go through the gate and straight up the hill field, to reach the track at the top.

Now follow the track. If you are tall, you will have a good view of the steam train if it passes. If you aren't tall, then a little further along the road, you will be able to see it. When you reach the road, cross straight over to pick up the trail directly on the other side, and now follow this trail under trees, keeping the fence to your left.

It will curve you around a bit, then when you reach the road, cross straight over and into the field on the other side.

Now follow the right perimeter of the field. You will reach an opening into another field on the right, but stay in this field, and then follow it as it curves to the right just ahead. There is a wide obvious grassy trail through here. You might also see some deer about.

When you reach a little bridge, go over it, and you will now be on a narrow dirt trail, and soon alongside a little river. Stay following the trail (there is only one so you can't get lost), and you will reach a big manor house with a moat. This is Groombridge Place. It's very fancy looking.

Now walk to the left over the little bridge, and a short way along at the road curve, you should see a trail straight ahead. Go along it, and this will lead you to a large green. Continue straight across it and you will reach the Groombridge Village Hall.

If you want a pub, turn left here and you will reach the Junction Inn, or turn right and you will reach the Crown Inn.

Walk to Birchden Wood

Continue straight across the road past the village store. This is an uphill residential street. Keep going all the way to the top, past the church, then there is a trail on the left just past the school.

This will lead you across a bridge with old train carriages below. Be careful on this bridge if you do this walk in winter. It can get icy and I've accidentally done the splits.

Past the trains, it's a narrow dirt track, and potentially lots of mud, to reach the road. There is a big trail arrow here telling you to go left. Ignore that and turn right. This will lead you into Birchden Wood.

The woods and Harrison's Rocks

Stay on the road as you enter, then when you reach the bend where it leads to the car park, stay straight though the big barrier.

It's quite lovely through here, surrounded by big trees. It's a nice wide obvious trail too… for now. This is one of the spots where you might lose your phone signal. It's mixed. Sometimes I've had good signal, sometimes nothing.

When you reach the junction, turn right, and stay on this trail as it takes you a bit under woods at first and then around the perimeter of the woods. The trail is now going to become a bit more off-piste, and potentially very muddy.

At some point there will be a gate on the left with a sign saying 'Harrison's Rocks'. Go through the gate and turn right, and this will lead you to the really cool big rock outcrops.

When you think the rocks have ended, they haven't. They come back, and keep going for some time, getting bigger and more impressive as you go along.

Stay on this same trail all the way through, which might be a little overgrown in parts, all the way to a more open area with a gate on the right. Go through the gate, and continue to the left. The trail will lead you onto a road, with an oast house ahead. Continue straight on this, and past some more houses to get back onto the trail.

Now follow this all the way to the end where there is a stile and gate. Pick which one you want, and you will reach the track and Pinstraw Farm.

Walk to Eridge Rocks

Follow the track to reach the main road, then turn right. This is Eridge Road. You are nearly at the rocks. Continue down the hill on this road, passing a house with silver birch trees, and after a few hundred meters you will reach a stile and trail signpost on the left. There is no pavement as you make your way there, so keep tight to the edge.

Go over the stile and follow the trail which will lead you over a series of two wooden bridges to reach a very, very large crop field.

Now, you might see a trail leading straight ahead, but the signs direct you to the right, and then left to walk through the crops.

I'd suggest walking along a trail as opposed to trampling over crops. You should asses the situation when you are there, and follow a trail which takes you to the other side of the field.

This field can be tough if it's muddy, and will take you a lot longer to get to the other side than you think.

When you do make it to the other side, you will hit the road. Turn right onto it, then take the second left dirt trail. It's the one with the hidden trail sign.

After potential lots of mud, you will reach the road, and the entrance to Eridge Rocks will be on the left. Now go and explore inside.

Walk to Frant

When you have finished, come back to the entrance, and turn left on the road, and follow it all the way to the other end where you will reach a main road, where you turn right.

A short way down the road, look out for a small metal gate into a field on the left, and now continue along the left edge of it, first downhill then uphill, then downhill again. Be careful of this field. I got chased by sheep here.

When you reach the little bridge, cross over, to get onto a narrow dirt trail. Then when you reach the road, cross over it and turn right into the woods.

You can't venture off this trail. Everything around you is private and there are many signs warning you of that. It might get a little confusing, but it's not for too long. Just make sure to keep the road to your right, but don't walk on it… yet.

You will eventually be led onto that road, which you are now allowed to walk on, and it's now more of a track. It will lead you out in the open, surrounded by lots of fields, with nice views. When you reach the end with big gates, the trail is almost hidden just to the left of them. Follow the trail, then turn right when you reach the trail signpost.

When you reach a gate that's like a door, go through it and turn left, with the big pond (or lake) to your right. When you reach a stream of water, walk over the bridge, and turn right. I didn't notice the bridge the first time. and thought I was going to have to walk through it.

You are now going to be walking surrounded by trees, passing a 'halfway-ish' sign. It's quite lovely with a touch of lonesome and mud (and probably no phone signal).

When you reach a field at the end, follow the trail to the left side of it, with the fence to your right. There is more potential for deer spotting here. You will then be led into a field, where you will see some houses up a hill ahead. That's Frant. And yes, you will need to walk up a hill to get to it.

Continue straight across the field, maybe spotting some more deer. At the other end of the field, you will reach a big gate. Go through it and turn left, then right a few meters along at the trail signpost. Now for the uphill.

When you reach the road turn left, and you will enter Frant.

At the big green, go onto it, past the pillbox, and over the little side road onto the next green.

Keep going up, onto another green (yes, there are a few of them), and follow the road that's called High Street. This will lead you past the George Inn, where you can stop for some pub time. There are just a few miles left to go.

Walk to Tunbridge Wells

Past the George Inn, you will reach the church. Go into it and follow the trail through on the right, and through a gate out the other end into a field. You will have a view to Tunbridge Wells from here.

Continue straight down this field, through some bushes, and into another field.

Continue straight down in the same direction, crossing over a path, to reach a mini gate into some woods.

Through the woods, when you reach the junction, turn left, then at the next junction take the right, and then a right at the one after. When you get to a little bridge, cross over, and you will next be on a very narrow trail with some overgrowth, and a field to the right. When you reach the end with a house ahead, turn left, then take the first right which is just after, and now follow this road through a farm.

At the main road, go straight across it and through the mini gate, and now continue straight along the edge of the field with a wall to your left and buildings ahead. Past the buildings and car park, you'll reach a main road, where you turn left.

Follow this road now for a few hundred meters, then look out for a trail sign on the right, which will lead you through some woods. As you near the end, there is a wooden structure which you might think you need to limbo under, but actually, as you get closer you will see you can walk through it.

You will then reach a road. A busy, noisy road. Turn right here, and at some point you need to figure out how to get across it.

When you do make it across, along the left side there will be a big wooden gate door to get you into a nice big green, away from the road.

When you enter, turn right and walk across it to reach the gate exit on the other side. Through the gate, cross the road (this one is easier), and you should see a trail and trail sign ahead to the left. Take that. It's called 'The Chase'.

When you reach the road end, the trail continues straight across just to the right.

At the next road, turn left, and follow it as it then curves right, then further ahead when it curves left, stay straight to get into a big green. This is 'The Grove'.

Now continue walking in the same direction along a path, and when you reach the other side, leave the green to go along a side residential street, and this will lead you onto the same high street from the start of the walk.

Turn right here and you will reach the station.

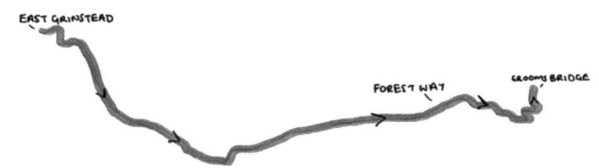

WALK 21

The Forest Way: East Grinstead to Groombridge

The Forest Way is a walking trail along an old railway line, taking you through the High Weald. I first heard about it from a patient at work, so I had to go and give it a go.

The whole walk is just how it sounds, lined with trees, like a forest. I was worried it might be a little tedious or monotonous, but I found it quite the opposite. I thoroughly enjoyed this walk, as the trees and their formations change as you go along, and at various points there are lovely views through the gaps.

The further you go, the more wild it feels. At times, when I was surrounded by the thick tree tunnel with the sounds of birds chirping, it felt a little rainforest-like.

You can visit Pooh Corner which is a cafe and museum with all things Pooh Bear. They have teddy bear toast.

WHAT TO EXPECT

Out of the station it's just under 1 mile to reach the trail, through the historic town of East Grinstead, which apparently has the longest row of medieval houses in Britain.

Once you make it to the trail, you are straight on a wide, slightly rugged path lined with trees, and it's like this the whole way. An easy, level, wide path, with the occasional road crossing, and lots of scenic view benches.

The first stop, about 2.5 miles in, is Forest Row where you can get refreshments if needed.

The next village, about 4 miles further in, is Hartfield, where the author of Winnie the Pooh is from. This walk doesn't take you into Hartfield, but it's a fun little extra if you like Winnie the Pooh stuff. You can visit Pooh Corner which is a cafe and museum with all things Pooh Bear. They have teddy bear toast. It will add about 1 mile to the walk.

Then after more trees, you finish at Groombridge, which has a steam train, and a couple of pubs. This walk is a little different from the others, in that it doesn't finish at a train station, you will need to get a bus back to East Grinstead. There is a station a couple of miles away in Ashurst. I walked to it once, and regretted it. Get the bus.

That first time, I wish I had stopped, but I kept going to get to Ashurst Station. This involved lots of mud (I was wearing white trainers), confusing woods, having to crouch under the overgrowth, non-existent trails, and having to go back on myself to find another way, falling into sharp bushes, and big fields exposed to the intense summer heatwave heat. Plus I missed the train and had to wait 45 min for the next one.

FUN FACT:
Forest Row was the inspiration for a Sherlock Holmes short story. Some big famous people have also lived here, such as David Gilmore (Pink Floyd) and Jimmy Page (Led Zeppelin).

DIRECTORY

LOGISTICS:

Start/Finish: East Grinstead Station, Groombridge. East Sussex.
Difficulty: Easy route, but moderate distance.
Type: Point to point.
Route Distance: 11 miles/17.5 km.
Time: 3–4h.

HOW TO GET THERE:

Direct trains from London Victoria to East Grinstead, 1h journey time. In Groombridge, there is a bus stop, with buses (the 291) back to East Grinstead.

COMING BY CAR:

Pay car park in Forest Row (Lower road car park) RH18 5DN. Then pick up the walk from there. The stretch after Forest Row is the best bit.

ELEVATION GAIN:

Flat, but if you walk into Hatfield, there is a small hill.

TERRAIN:

Wide dirt path, road.

DOG FRIENDLY:

Yes.

PHONE SIGNAL:

Yes.

PUBLIC TOILETS:

Yes, in East Grinstead Station. Only along the route if you stop somewhere to eat.

IDEAL TIME OF YEAR:

Summer is perfect as you will be sheltered from the heat by the trees. Or autumn for the autumn leaves.

OPTION TO SHORTEN THE WALK:

Yes. Forest Row 4 miles, Hatfield 7.5 miles. Each have buses back to East Grinstead. The 291 from both, and 270 or 261 from Forest Row.

WHERE TO EAT?

A number of options along the route, and plenty of options in East Grinstead.

CAFE AND COFFEE:

East Grinstead

- The Mug Tea Room (dog friendly).
- 1 Middle Row Cafe (dog friendly).

On the walk

- 4 miles: Emilio's Coffee, Forest Row (dog friendly).
- 4 miles: Hop Yard Brewing Co, Forest Row (dog friendly).
- 7.5 miles: Pooh Corner Cafe, Hartfield (dogs allowed in tea garden).
- 7.5 miles: Mobile Coffee Truck, Hartfield (dog friendly).

PUB:

The Crown Inn or The Junction Inn, in Groombridge. Both dog friendly.

FOR SUPPLIES:

Supermarkets in East Grinstead, Tesco Express in Forest Row, The village bakery in Groombridge.

TIPS/OTHER THINGS TO KNOW

- It's hard ground the whole way, so wear comfortable shoes/trainers. I don't recommend hiking boots for this one.
- The Forest Way is actually route 21 of the cycle network. You can hire bikes at Forest Row with a smartphone unlocking system. Just download the app, turn up, and pick up a bike. No booking required. You will find the bikes in the community centre car park. You can find all the info on the Forest Row government website.
- There are picnic benches at various points along the route if you need a break.

More bridges being claimed by nature. More views through the trees. It's very peaceful.

ROUTE DESCRIPTION

Out of East Grinstead Station, follow the signs to the town centre. When you reach the high street, turn right and keep going to the end where you will see some medieval buildings. Turn left here.

As you walk along the high street, it's lined with them. So many. You need to keep going, past all the shops, and keep going some more down the road. Further than you think. You will eventually see the Forest Way signs pointing to a trail on the right. Follow it.

Walk to Forest Row

Now it's as simple as following the trail. Early on there is a road crossing, but then it's just pure woodland trail for a good while.

You will be able to see some views through the trees, and for part of the walk, the trail is on a ridge, with big drops down the sides.

At some point you will come across a little trail to the right up the bank. This is optional if you want to mix things up. It's more rugged up there, and the views are ok. I personally don't think it's worth the uphill, but you might like it, it's all subjective. It will lead you back onto this main trail anyway.

After a couple more road crossings and lots more trees, you will reach a main road. You can turn right to walk into Forest Row (if you want to stop there), or stay on the path for a little longer and take the right turn when you see the Forest Row sign nestled in the hedge. Either way, you will now walk on the road to reach it. It's alright. Some cute buildings, a quaint village hall, some eating places, and a green but I would only pop over there if you want something to eat, are interested in the history, or are planning to finish the walk here.

If you ventured over to Forest Row, to get back to the Forest Way trail, walk across the green onto the big obvious trail, then at the junction, turn left which will lead you to the Forest Way.

When you reach the main trail, there is a sculpture thing. You will see these at various points along the trail. It is one of 1000 funded by the Royal Bank of Scotland, to mark the millennium and the creation of the cycle network.

Walk to Hartfield

Turn right now on the trail, and keep going. I feel that the trail gets better along here. It is all still just one long wide straight path lined with trees, but the trees change the most now. Sometimes tighter and more bush like, other times tall and big, changing the shape of the tree tunnel.

More bridges being claimed by nature. More views through the trees. It's very peaceful. The times I've been here have been summer weekends, and there has been barely anyone else around. The occasional cyclist maybe, and even less walkers. It feels so away from everything.

You will at some point reach the road with a sign pointing right to Hartfield. If you want to see Winnie the Pooh stuff, head up there. It's about a 5 or 10 min walk (with a bit of a hill) to reach Pooh Corner.

To stay on the trail, go left, then take the first right back onto the trail.

Walk to Groombridge

This section is out in the open for a moment, which is a nice but brief change from tree cover. Then it's back under. More trees, some wild garlic. The smell gives it away. There is also a view to some pointy cone roofed buildings (oast houses), a war pillbox, and some grand homes. It's a bit more flowery through here as well.

When you reach the main road, cross straight over to get onto the trail, and after a little bit more woodland, the trail takes you out in the open to reach the next road. The trees are finished now.

Cross this road, to pick up the trail opposite, and follow the pretty path as it winds along to the next road. From here, follow the sign left to Groombridge. It's a road without a pavement, but not car heavy.

Keep following this road as it curves to the right, then left, passing by the church.

At the bottom of the road, bear left (or turn right if you want to find one of the pubs), then turn right on the main road, and the bus stop is next to the red telephone box. To go to the other pub, continue on, past another church to the row of buildings up the hill.

PUBLIC TRANSPORT

The northern part of the Kent Downs is better connected by train than the southern part. These are the trains used for the walks in the book, with a journey time ranging from 35 min to 1h30min.

London Bridge – Southeastern

Charing Cross – Southeastern

London Victoria – Southeastern

Blackfriars – Thameslink

London St Pancras – Southeastern

WALK 22
Wye to Devil's Kneading Trough
5 miles

WALK 23
Shoreham circular via Otford
8 miles

WALK 24
Knole Park and Ingtham Mote
11 miles

KENT DOWNS NATIONAL LANDSCAPE

Known as the garden of England, the Kent Downs is very pretty and a bit more posh in places than the others.

Stretching from the Surrey Hills in the west, down to the rugged White cliffs of Dover in the south, with quaint historic villages, bluebells, ancient woodland, white chalk hill figures, and rolling hills in between. Also known for the distinctive coned shaped roofed oast houses used for drying hops, some dating back to the 15th century.

Designated an AONB (now National Landscape) in 1968, it covers 326 square miles.

The North Downs Way also runs through here, stretching for 153 miles from Farnham on the west side of the Surrey Hills, and finishing down in Dover.

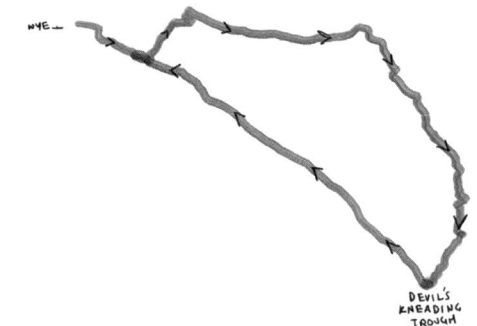

WALK 22

Wye to Devil's Kneading Trough

This is a really easy route to follow, taking you from the medieval village of Wye to a deep crater known as Devil's Kneading Trough, in the Wye National Nature Reserve.

You'll see a surprise chalk hill figure, walk through straggly ancient woods with fallen trees, and follow a trail along a ridge over the chalk grassland with just the most incredible magnificent views.

The man I bought some cheese from in Wye told me that on a clear day you can see France from up there. I think he was joking, but you can see so far that it wouldn't surprise me.

Then of course there is Devil's Kneading Trough. It's an uphill climb to reach the top of it, which is breathy and involves some steps, but it's not too long.

Now, I've had a good search as to what the Devil story is for this one, and all I can find is that if you walk around it seven times then drink water from the natural spring, you will see the Devil. If you give it a go, let me know what happens.

At the top, you will be on the edge of the crater valley which you can now walk around.

WHAT TO EXPECT

You basically walk in straight lines. A straight line all the way to reach it, then a straight-ish line all the way back.

Out of Wye, it's your usual trails taking you along the edges of fields. This is where you'll get a view of the chalk crown. As I said, you are just walking in a straight line, all the way to reach the road and the entrance to the Wye National Nature Reserve. Then it's that hill. You'll head straight up, and it's pretty steep, but as you get higher the views will open up, giving you that oomph to keep going.

At the top, you will be on the edge of the crater valley which you can now walk around. To get back, you'll walk along the top of the hill now, following the North Downs Way, in a straight line again, with a view out to the horizon. You'll pass the chalk crown, then it's a short bit through some wild woods, before turning to head downhill back to Wye.

FUN FACT:
Fossilised shark teeth have been found in the area. Many millions of years ago this site was under the sea.

DIRECTORY

LOGISTICS:

Start/Finish: Wye Station, Kent.
Difficulty: Easy.
Type: Circular.
Route Distance: Just over 5 miles/ 8 km.
Time: 2–3h.

HOW TO GET THERE:

Direct train from London Bridge (or Charing Cross), on Southeastern. Journey time: 1h20min–1h30min.
Or from London St Pancras it's 55min with a change at Ashford International.

COMING BY CAR:

You can park by the Devil's Kneading Trough at the Wye Nature Reserve car park, TN25 5HE. It was free, but I've now heard you have to pay, using RingoApp. I would still do this full walk into Wye and back, because it's such a quaint village that you need to see. You can follow the route description starting from the Trough.

ELEVATION GAIN:

203m/666ft.

TERRAIN:

Grass, mud, dirt trail.

DOG FRIENDLY:

Yes. No stiles. Some livestock could be about, so just be aware of that.

PHONE SIGNAL:

Yes.

PUBLIC TOILETS:

Yes, in the village.

IDEAL TIME OF YEAR:

Anytime is great. Might just be a bit muddy after rain.

OPTION TO SHORTEN THE WALK:

No.

WHERE TO EAT?

Nothing along the route, but a few options in Wye.

CAFE AND COFFEE:

Wye

- The Hub (dog friendly).
- Wye Coffee Shop and Kitchen (dog friendly).

PUB:

Wye

- The Tickled Trout Pub (dog friendly).

FOR SUPPLIES:

Wye Wholefoods, Co-op.

TIPS/OTHER THINGS TO KNOW

- There is a trail that takes you through the middle of the valley, which has unexploded ordnance. Don't worry, this route doesn't take you along there. I'm surprised it's open to the public. There is a sign saying that you take full responsibility if something happens to you in there.
- Hiking boots recommended.
- Limited spaces at the car park. There is a lay-by type place you can park further along the road as well.

Walk 22

ROUTE DESCRIPTION

Out of the station, turn left. If you have arrived from London direction, you will walk over the railway lines. Now it's super simple, you just continue walking in this straight direction through town, passing by the pub, and some medieval residential houses. It's about 2 miles to reach the nature reserve from here.

When the road curves to the left, turn right (or rather, stay straight) onto Cherry Garden Lane. It's where the road signs are nestled in the hedge.

Now continue along this path where it's a mix of residential and hedge and bush lined, then alongside the edge of a field. In this field, you will get a view to the North Downs ridge of the Kent Downs, and a crown chalk hill figure. This is the Wye Memorial Crown.

It was created to celebrate the coronation of King Edward VII in 1902.

FUN FACT:
It was covered up during WWII to prevent it being used for navigation by enemy aircraft.

Walk to the Wye National Nature Reserve

You'll then be on a road and car parking area for a moment, then when the road curves to the right, you stay straight again to get onto a track. You should see a trail sign here.

Continue along this track with more views to the crown, then when you reach the road, cross straight over again, to pick up the trail on the other side. This will then lead you along the left edge of a large crop field.

At the other end, continue through the gap in the bushes ahead just on the left, but when you enter the next field, there are actually two, separated by bushes and trees. Take the field on the left, but still walk in the same direction you got here, so you will be walking along the right edge of the field, but now with bush and trees to your right. It can get very muddy and slippery through here.

At the end of this field, continue straight through the middle of the next one, then on the other side, go through some bushes on the left. This will lead you to the road. Turn right on the road, then to the left a few meters along enter the Wye National Nature Reserve.

Walk up to Devil's Kneading Trough

Go through the gate, and up the hill, then when you reach another gate, don't go that way. That will take you along the route with the unexploded ordnance.

Instead, continue up the hill to the left, to reach another gate. Go through this one.

Now you just continue up. It's a mix of steps and trail, narrow and winding.

As you get higher up, you will start to see the deep valley crater opening up to your right, and some insane views behind.

When you reach the top, you aren't quite at the top yet. This is the Millstone viewpoint. It's quite a view. Looking out across a flat landscape, disappearing miles into the horizon.

Now, continue along the wide grass path to reach a gate. For the way back, you will take the trail on the left through the gate. For now, continue straight to walk around the top of Devil's Kneading Trough.

The woods and the North Downs Way

When you have finished exploring, go back to that gate to follow the trail. You will now be following the North Downs Way all the way back to Wye, sort of. I'll explain in a minute.

So, following this trail, you'll go through a gate and along the left edge of a field, then at the junction, take the trail to the left through another gate and into woods briefly. When you reach the next junction, take the right which will lead you to a gate and the road.

Cross straight over the road, onto the road opposite, where you will see a sign for the Big Coombe Farm. A few meters along take the left through a gate, and now follow the trail along the hilltop. It's really magnificent along here. A view along the edge as it drops down below, and those vast far reaching views again.

You're going to be following this all the way until you reach some woods. It's a bit under 1/2 a mile.

Now, when you reach the woods, the North Downs Way sign will tell you to turn right. Ignore that, and stay straight to enter the woods. It's very wild in here, with a few trees and branches you will need to limbo under. Now, keep going through the woods until you reach a junction (note: just before the junction is a small trail to the right, don't take that one).

At the junction you should see a North Downs Way sign, this is where you join it again. So follow it to the left, and now you will walk downhill through the woods, with maybe a fallen tree obstacle along the way. It can get a bit slippy down here.

Walk back to Wye

The trail will lead you out of the woods, and along the right edge of a field, still going downhill. Now you just continue in this straight line, through some fields, all the way back to Wye.

When you reach the village, you will be on the outskirts through a car parking area. Keep going to reach the road, then walk to the left of the big brick building ahead. Just past there, take the trail on the left. This will lead you to an allotment, where you turn left.

Past the allotment you will walk through the church grounds.

When you reach the road, you should continue along the road straight ahead. It's quite something. You'll find some very old buildings along here, the shop I bought the cheese from, and further along where the cars aren't parked, it feels a little like walking in a movie set.

At the end of this road, if you turn right, this will lead you to the pub and back to the station.

WALK 23

Shoreham circular via Otford

This is a fantastic walk across the Darent Valley, featuring a Site of Special Scientific Interest, a chalk hill figure, woodland, and two medieval villages. There are views that take your breath away (well, they took mine anyway), including a view to the skyscrapers of London.

One of those villages is Otford. It's quite a place. A heritage village, with its history on full show. Centuries old cottages, a Grade II listed duck pond (the only listed duck pond in the country), and apparently one of the largest scale models of the Solar System in the world.

The walk is quite hilly too.

One of the great things about this walk, is that if you don't think you are fit enough for an 8 miler, you can split it in two, as there is a train station at the halfway mark. The two halves are quite different, and each has a pub (or two) to finish.

*Always love
an oast
house.*

WHAT TO EXPECT

The Shoreham to Otford half is the most hilly, the most wild, and potentially the most muddy. The Otford to Shoreham half still has a big hill, but it's just the one. The rest is super easy both in difficulty and in navigation.

To start, you have a hill straight away, through woods, then things level out across some fields and a farm to reach Magpie Bottom. A Site of Scientific Special Interest, and one of the most spectacular things I've seen. The view down into the valley is truly breathtaking. It's then a big downhill, followed by a big uphill, a cool tree tunnel in between, and then a view to the skyscrapers of London.

After a few more fields, one of which may or may not have a bull inside (more on that later), you'll walk through some wild woods to reach the road. It's then a bit of road to walk, to reach the next field, and then you'll get a view down to Otford as you make your descent.

FUN FACT:

Do you know of Samuel Palmer? I didn't. He's quite a key figure in the world of painting (from the 19th Century). He lived in Shoreham and would paint the landscapes here.

From Otford, the remainder of the walk is mostly flat across a few fields with a view to the Shoreham Cross in the distance, passing by an oast house. Always love an oast house. There's then one sneaky uphill, with great views by the way, to reach the Shoreham Cross. From there you can descend into the village to finish.

DIRECTORY

LOGISTICS:

Start/Finish: Shoreham Station. Kent.
Difficulty: Moderate.
Type: Circular.
Route Distance: 8 miles/13 km.
Time: 3–4h.

HOW TO GET THERE:

Direct trains from Blackfriars, journey time 1h. Or indirect trains from London Bridge, journey time 37min or Victoria, journey time 50min.

COMING BY CAR:

There is the Filston Lane car park in Shoreham, TN14 7SP, which is free. In Otford there is the village car park which is pay and display, but very reasonably priced (at the time of writing anyway).

ELEVATION GAIN:

415m/1362ft.

TERRAIN:

Dirt trail, tracks, mud, some road, grass, steps, stiles.

DOG FRIENDLY:

Yes, with some precautions. Some livestock about, a bit of road walking. The stiles all have doggy sized holes.

PHONE SIGNAL:

Yes, mostly. I find in parts of Shoreham it can vanish.

PUBLIC TOILETS:

Yes, at Otford Station only.

IDEAL TIME OF YEAR:

Spring for all the meadow flowers.

OPTION TO SHORTEN THE WALK:

Yes. Otford, 4 miles in, has a train station. You could choose to finish the walk here, or even start from here and do the second part of the walk into Shoreham.

WHERE TO EAT?

The options in Shoreham are better than Otford.

CAFE AND COFFEE:

Shoreham
- Honey Pot Cafe and Tea Rooms (dog friendly).
- The Old Bakery Tea Room (dog friendly).

PUB:

Shoreham
- The Kings Arms (dog friendly).
- The Crown (dog friendly).
- The Samuel Palmer (dog friendly).

Otford
- The Bull (dog friendly).

RESTAURANTS:

Shoreham

• The Mount Vineyard (dog friendly).

TIPS/OTHER THINGS TO KNOW

• Can get very muddy in winter, after lots of rain.

• Hiking boots recommended.

• There is one field that may have a bull in. I've never seen it, so don't panic. If it's there, you can skirt along the perimeter of the field.

> *I suspect some
> of the mud
> is also cow poo.*

ROUTE DESCRIPTION

Out of the station, head through the car parking area to reach the main road.

The trail is just to the right of the house you should see on the other side of the road. There are actually two trails there. Take the one that leads straight up the hill.

It's a solid uphill now along a dirt trail, and you should pass an interesting Nature Reserve sign on a tree. Apparently there are adders about. Best not think about that too much.

When you reach a junction, take the left trail, which is nice and level, giving you a momentary break from the hill (the hills return soon).

You will be walking through woods, which get more wild as you go along.

Then you reach the steps. Lots of steps up. If there are no leaves on the trees, you might get a peak to the Shoreham Cross if you look back.

The farm

Keep going up, crossing the junction, all the way to reach a field. Now walk straight across it, towards the farm on the other side.

At the farm, continue straight through, and then do a small right and left, to reach the track. It can get very muddy through here by the way. I suspect some of the mud is also cow poo.

The track will take you downhill, then up again, with nice views across the surrounding valley fields, then once up the other side, you will reach a trail leading off it to the left through a field. Take it, to walk diagonally through the field, which might have some corn, then when you reach the next field, follow the trail to the right towards the trees.

Magpie Bottom

Under the trees you will now go downhill, which gets quite steep, with a view to a big hill through the trees ahead. Yes, you have to walk all the way down to then go up that one.

Once you exit the trees you get a proper view of it. And what a view it is. Down into the valley. It feels a bit like you've uncovered a little secret. Some hidden land. This is Magpie Bottom, a Site of Special Scientific Interest.

Now, if you look down the hill to the left, you should see a gate at the bottom. Head down to that.

Through the gate you will walk through a really cool tree tunnel, which I'm pleased to report goes on for quite some time.

Once out of the trees, go straight up the hill. This is that hill. It's hard work, but it doesn't go on for too long. At the top, make sure to look back at the views. Now from the other side of the valley.

The trail will now lead you to a stile and into another meadow, with a mini hill. After the one you just did, it won't feel like a hill.

When up the hill, if you look back you will get a view to London. The skyscrapers of Canary Wharf. When I first walked here, I wasn't expecting that. I only looked back to see the wonderful meadow view, and let out a gasp when I saw it.

More fields and Great Wood

You'll now go over another stile, and along an alley type of path, then take the first right turn.

When you reach the gate, through it you will be presented with a stile and a gate ahead. Don't take the gate, take the stile into a field, and continue along the left edge of it. There can be livestock here. I've not seen them, but there is evidence of them by way of a trough.

At the other end, the trail curves to the left, but stay straight to go over a stile and into another field. You'll now walk along the right edge of this field, and partway along go through the wooden fence type thing which leads you along a dirt trail downhill to the road.

At the road turn left, then a few meters along, turn right to go over a stile into a field. Now, this is a bull field. There is a big sign warning you of that. However, I've never seen a bull in here. You need to now walk across this field, at about 11 o'clock. For safety, I like to walk around the left edge, so I have an escape if Mr Bull is present. The escape is sharp bushes, and barbed wire. But I'll take that over the bull.

On the other side of this field, go through a big gate, and then a diagonal left down the hill towards the woodland. In the woods, just follow the trail straight through. I can't find any info about these woods, but they look like they could be ancient. Very wild and scraggly.

Walk to Otford

Out the other side, turn right onto the road. There is now a bit of a walk on this road without a path, probably a bit under 1/2 a mile. I don't find it too bad though, and it's a scenic road lined with trees.

When you reach a corner with another road joining this one, go straight through the middle to enter a field. Stay straight along the left edge of this field, which will lead you into some more woods. Then out the other side you will have a lovely view down to Otford. Now walk downhill heading towards the view.

At the bottom, turn right along the road.

Just on the left here is the Otford Chalk Pit. You used to be able to walk through there, which then leads you to Otford Station, but sinkholes started appearing so it's been closed off for now.

So instead, continue along the road, then take a left at the end and you will reach the station. Look out for an oast house as you walk along this bit.

If you stay on this road, you will reach Otford, but there is a nicer way to get there. Go down the steps as if you are going to the station, then walk through the car park, and about halfway along, there is a path to the right.

This path will lead you to Otford village centre, with some nice meadows and a dreamy cottage to look at along the way.

Otford

You could definitely spend some time exploring around here. There are information boards dotted about, telling you about the history of all the buildings you are seeing. You don't even have to veer too much off course, you will pass the history along the way.

That listed duck pond I mentioned earlier? That will be right in front of you when you arrive. In the middle of the roundabout. This used to be the main supply of clean water for the village.

FUN FACT:
There used to be edible frogs in the pond, but they disappeared once the ducks were introduced in the 1950's.

Continue along the road on the other side of the roundabout from where you arrived, passing by some more medieval buildings, with information boards. You'll pass The Bull Inn, which dates back to the 1400's. Back then it was a house.

Then you reach Pickmoss Cottage, which stands out with its Tudor facade. This is where you turn right, alongside the stream.

Walk to the Shoreham Cross

Continue along the stream very briefly, before taking the trail which you will see ahead on the right. This will lead you to a big field, with a view to the Shoreham Cross in the distance ahead.

Follow the trail along the left side of the field, and you are now going to be walking in a rough straight line for the next mile or so. Through a few fields, and gates, then through the woods, with a golf course to your left. When you reach the road, turn left. There are actually two lefts. Don't take the golf course left, take the road left. It's a very narrow track type road, but quite scenic and not car heavy. Unfortunately it takes you downhill, which means you have a bigger uphill in a minute. Fortunately you get to see another oast house at the bottom.

The road will then lead you straight onto the trail, where you then cross over a little bridge and continue alongside the river for a bit. When you reach the road, the uphill begins. It's gentle at first, then at the road junction, continue straight over to pick up the trail just to the left, and keep going up. It gets steeper now. When you reach the field, it becomes even steeper, for the final push to the top. Luckily, you don't have to walk all the way to the top. When you reach a bench, and gate on the right, you can stop there.

Make sure to look back at the views. The reward for your hard work.

Through the gate, it's all easy for the rest of the walk. Following the trail, it's surrounded by trees at first, then things start to open up to the right for a wonderful view to Shoreham below.

After about 1/2 a mile, there will be an opening to the right where you will find the Shoreham Cross. The Shoreham Cross was dug in 1920 in memory of those who lost their lives in WWI. You can't really see it properly, as you are right on it, that comes later. There is a bench here though, for sitting and admiring the view.

Walk to Shoreham

You have two options to get back to Shoreham from here. If you want to keep going for a little longer, go back onto the trail and keep following it right to the very end. You will get to enjoy the views for a bit longer this way. Then when you reach the end with a road, turn right to walk down along the edge of a field. When you reach a gate, go through it, and this will lead you down to the village. When you get there, turn right and you will reach The Crown Inn.

For the more direct way to get down to Shoreham, go through the gate by the cross, and go diagonally down the hill to reach the gate at the bottom. Then continue straight down and you will arrive. When you get there, left will take you to The Crown Pub, right will take you to the Honey Pot Cafe and Tea Rooms.

To get back to the station, turn right, then take the first left, and follow this road all the way over the bridge, to reach the church. You will pass by The Kings Arms along here.

Go under the arch and along the path lined with trees through the church graveyard, then through the black gate on the other side, turn right onto the path. This will lead you to the station. Make sure to look back just before you reach the station for the best view to the Shoreham Cross.

Shoreham circular via Otford

WALK 24

Knole Park and Ingtham Mote

This is a very pretty walk, and very easy to navigate, think lots of straight lines, taking you across the Kent Downs. It's very hilly though, but with hills comes the views. Incredible far reaching views. It also features deer, and two National Trust properties. Knole House and Ingtham Mote.

Knole House, part of a 600-year-old estate, is a grand manor, once home to Archbishops and royalty (Henry VIII time).

Ingtham Mote is a 14th century manor house surrounded by a moat and gardens. It is perfectly preserved and one of the oldest surviving medieval manor houses in England.

There is so much history to both of these places, far too much to describe here, but you can read more about it on the National Trust website.

You do have to pay if you want to visit inside the properties, however, this isn't mandatory for the walk. The route takes you around the outside of them, which is still great in itself, seeing the impressive buildings from the outside. The medieval Ingtham Mote is sort of hidden and tucked away, then suddenly revealing itself as you walk over the hill, and the grand Knole House in the middle of a massive park.

The whole area is also very horsey. Lots of horse fields.

WHAT TO EXPECT

From the station, it's about a 20min walk to reach Knole Park. After which you walk all the way to the other side, along a nice laid out path, uphill, probably spotting some deer along the way.

Out the other end, it's a bit of woodland, downhill now, to reach the Bucks Head pub. Then it's a bit of quaint country road walking, more woods, some fields, apple trees, and a lavender farm, to reach Ingtham Mote.

From there you make your way back, this time with all the views, lots more hills, and enchanting woods. The trail back is more rugged, and more muddy. Then you finish off back through Knole Park and to Knole House.

The whole area is also very horsey. Lots of horse fields.

FUN FACT:

If you are a Beatles fan, you might be interested to know that Strawberry Fields and Penny Lane's music videos have been shot in Knole Park.

DIRECTORY

LOGISTICS:

Start/Finish: Sevenoaks Station, Kent.
Difficulty: Moderate.
Type: Circular.
Route Distance: 11 miles/17.5 km.
Time: 4–5h.

HOW TO GET THERE:

Direct trains from London Bridge (or Charing Cross) to Sevenoaks on Southeastern. Fast train takes about 30 min.

COMING BY CAR:

Paid parking in Sevenoaks town centre TN13 1LW. You can park in the Knole car park, but only if you buy a ticket to visit the property.

ELEVATION GAIN:

425m/1394ft.

TERRAIN:

Grass, dirt trail, mud, road, one stile.

DOG FRIENDLY:

Dogs must be on a lead in the park, due to the deer. Otherwise it's dog friendly. The one stile is big and gappy.

PHONE SIGNAL:

Patchy. There are a few spots without signal.

PUBLIC TOILETS:

Yes. At Sevenoaks Station, Knole (if you have entry into the property), and at Ingtham Mote.

IDEAL TIME OF YEAR:

July for the lavender. Autumn for the colourful leaves.

OPTION TO SHORTEN THE WALK:

Not without skipping something. If you don't mind though, I would recommend following the route through Knole Park, to reach the Bucks Head pub, stop to eat, then turn back. This will be 5 miles.

WHERE TO EAT?

There is one pub along the route, but you are spoilt for choice in Sevenoaks. Here are some recommendations.

CAFE AND COFFEE:

Sevenoaks

- Beaux Bagels (for something on the go/ dog friendly).
- Life on High (dog friendly).
- Buntastic (dog friendly).

On the walk

- Both National Trust sites have a cafe, but it's only if you have entry into the properties.

PUB:

Sevenoaks

- The Anchor (dog friendly).
- The Restoration (dog friendly).

On the walk

- 2.5 miles: The Bucks Head, Godden Green (dog friendly).

FOR SUPPLIES:

Multiple supermarkets and convenience stores in Sevenoaks.

TIPS/OTHER THINGS TO KNOW

- Don't get too close to the deer, or try to feed them. If they are on your path, then walk around them keeping a wide berth.
- Knole Park will likely be very busy on summer weekends.
- If coming by car and parking at Knole (to visit the property), pre-booking is essential on weekends and during school holidays.
- At the time of writing, Knole offers 2 for 1 on admission to the property if you come car free.
- Hiking boots are recommended due to the mud and hills. If you plan to just walk through Knole Park, then trainers are fine.

> *This will lead you up the hill,
> through the trees, and then you will
> see Knole House ahead.*

ROUTE DESCRIPTION

Turn right out of the station, and make your way up the main road (which is uphill). When you reach the main junction, take either of the two forks ahead. If you take the left fork, this will lead you to the high street where you turn right. If you take the right fork, when you reach the shops, take one of the left turns and you will reach the high street, where you turn right.

Follow the high street, and look out for a left turn onto Akehurst Lane. It's next to the opticians.

At the end of the lane, to the right you should see a sign on the stone and brick wall saying 'Webb's Alley leading to Knole Park', and a path to the right of it. Go along that path.

Continue all the way downhill to the gate entrance to Knole Park.

It's quite a steep downhill, which means you will have to walk back uphill on the way back later, but that's a problem for later.

Walk through Knole Park

You will see a path straight ahead leading up the hill that will take you to Knole House. For this walk though, I will take you a slightly different way, as you come back via Knole House at the end.

After entering Knole Park, turn left into the wide grass valley. You might spot some deer along here. When you reach the main path, turn right onto it. This will lead you up the hill, through the trees, and then you will see Knole House ahead.

Knole was the Sackville family home for over 400 years, and in 1946 was gifted to the National Trust, with private apartments being leased back to the now Sackville-West family, who still own most of the parkland, deer and house contents.

Don't walk all the way up to it (unless you are planning to go inside), instead, after the curve in the path, you should see a grass type trail to the left. Walk along that, with a view to the golf course ahead in the distance.

Follow this grass path down the hill and you should see a proper path ahead, leading up a hill. You are walking to that. When you reach the path, continue on it all all the way to the other end of the park. You will be walking through a golf course here.

When you reach the very end with a gate, you need to go through it, but it's confusing. The first time I spent about 5min trying to figure it out, and when I gave up, someone turned up and told me how it works. So, there is a little gap to the right of it, but the gap is a dead end. Which is what confused me. In the gap, the gate on the left opens. That's what you go through.

Walk to the Bucks Head

Through the gate, you will enter Godden Wood. It's a nice wide dirt path leading you through, which can become a little muddy and is more rugged further along. It's about 1/2 a mile to reach Godden Green and the pub.

Just before the end of the woods, there is a trail split. Take the right one, and you will reach a road. The trail picks up straight across to the left of the building, past the horse stables, then at the very end you will reach the road and Godden Green. The Bucks Head pub is just to the right.

Walk to Ingtham Mote

Turn right on the road, with the pub and pond with duck house on the right, then at the fork, take the left one. You will be walking on a quiet road now for a bit. It's a nice road, passing by cottages, and in parts the road becomes more dirt-like.

Along this road, when you reach a fork, the left goes into someone's home, so take the right. After about 1/2 a mile you will be lead onto a small dirt trail through the bushes, and steeply downhill.

At the bottom, the trail will lead out then back under woods. When you see a 'private' gate on the right, stay on the trail as it curves to the left, then a short way along, stay on this trail as it curves to the right. This will lead you under a nice tree tunnel, with a field with horses on the right.

When you reach the road with a house ahead, turn right, then at the road T-junction, cross straight over to pick up the trail on the other side. This will lead you down the middle of some apple trees. When you reach the road with a triangle in the middle, walk onto the road straight across to the right. This feels more like a path road. First lined with trees, and then surrounded by fields. The lavender field is to the right.

Stay following this path, then when you reach a split, where it would seem like you turn left, don't turn left. Stay straight on the more dirt-like trail. At the very end of the field, stay straight to walk alongside the bushes, and then steeply downhill, surrounded by trees.

Stay on this main path all the way down, then at the junction with a pond ahead, turn left. You can now follow this path all the way to the road at the end, which is a bit under 1/2 a mile. It's a nice wide dirt path, and very easy to follow, and you will pass by a Hoppers Hut, belonging to Ingtham Mote, along the way.

When you reach the road, turn right, and after about 200m you will get your first view to Ingtham Mote.

Continue along the road, passing by the farm building on the right (remember this as you will walk up there later), and you will reach the gate entrance to Ingtham Mote on the left. It has had a number of owners, from squires, to sheriffs, and MPs. The last private owner was American business man, Charles Henry Robertson, who bequeathed it to the National Trust after his death in 1985.

Without paying, you can walk along the outside of the Ingtham Mote property (with a good view of it), but to go into the grounds and house, you will need to pay. If you continue along towards the National Trust entrance, there are some picnic benches, and various other trails you can explore for free.

Walk back to Knole Park

Walk back out and to the farm building you passed earlier, and turn left to walk past it.

When you reach the buildings with pointy roofs, turn right, and make your way uphill along the track. It's a big uphill climb now. But you know what uphill means… good views.

Stay on this main path all the way, past any junctions, and further up you will get some amazing far reaching views to the left.

After about 3/4 of a mile, you will reach some steps to the right. Go up them, and continue along the trail with even better views to the left. You will stay on this trail in a pretty straight direction now, which becomes a bit more rugged further along. When you reach the road, turn right for a steep (but short) uphill, to reach the Rooks Hill Cottage.

On the left side of the road here, you will see some steep rugged steps. Go up them.

It's another steep uphill, and then you will walk through a mass of woods, on a narrow trail with a steep drop to the left. This bit is extremely rugged and undulates a lot. When you reach the gate you will enter One Tree Hill.

Through the gate, turn right, then almost immediately left to now follow a wider dirt path. When you reach the grassy opening out of the woods, turn left and you will reach the One Tree Hill viewpoint, for more incredible far reaching views.

Nearly back at Knole Park now. From here, take the right trail (if you are facing the view), then at the trail split, take the left.

When you reach the road, turn left, then take the right up the drive towards Shepherds Mead. Just before the white gate, take the narrow trail to the right, up the hill (with more views), then when you see a gate and fence ahead, turn right then immediate left to go through the other gate. This will lead you into a horse area, with horse jumping stuff.

In this field, follow the perimeter straight ahead then right, and then partway along the edge of the field, look out for a stile to the left to enter the woods.

In the woods, follow the trail in a diagonal right, and this will lead you to the road with Knole Park straight ahead. When you enter Knole Park, continue in a straight direction and this will take you all the way to Knole House.

As you make your way there, when you cross over a main path, if you want to go and see the Beatles filming locations, turn right along the path. You will be able to see the spots marked on Google Maps. To get to Knole House, don't turn right. Stay straight.

Walk back to Sevenoaks

When you reach Knole House, walk around the front of it and along the path through the middle of the car park. Partway through, you want to turn left. There are footpath signs on the little wooden stumps on the ground to guide you. Follow these through the car park and over the grass hill.

Continue walking straight-ish (sometimes the trail isn't obvious, but there are little public footpath signs dotted about to guide you), and you will be led down the other side of the hill and back to the gate you entered Knole Park in.

Now it's that steep hill. This time you need to walk up it. Good luck.

At the top, walk to the right, then along the road to the left and you will be back on the high street.

You can now explore around the town, or make your way back to the station.

PUBLIC TRANSPORT

The South East coast is very well connected by trains in and out of London, including the high speed train, and you can walk almost the whole coast by walking from station to station. These walks are however, the furthest from London, and journey time ranges from 1h – 1h45min. These are the routes used in the book:

London St Pancras – Southeastern, Thameslink

London Victoria – Southern, Southeastern

London Bridge – Thameslink

Blackfriars – Thameslink

WALK 25
Margate to Ramsgate via Broadstairs
9 miles

WALK 26
Dover to Deal
11 miles

WALK 27
Seven Sisters
13.5 miles

WALK 28
Folkestone to Dover
9 miles

WALK 29
Newhaven to Brighton
11.5 miles

WALK 30
Herne Bay to Margate
12.5 miles

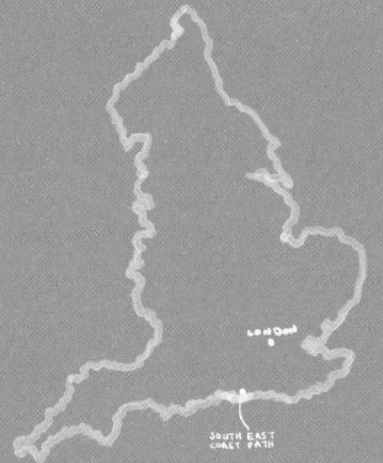

SOUTH EAST COAST PATH

The South East coast path is a bit of a mix. Some bits are hilly, and you have some impressive white chalk cliffs. You may have heard of the White Cliffs of Dover? Or what about the Seven Sisters? These aren't the only ones though. You will find more along the North Kent coast and further along the East Sussex coast.

There is also a lot of 'flat'. Whether along a promenade by a seaside town, or just in between places where there isn't really anything. Some bits are quite bleak, and you feel like you are at the end of nowhere.

The beaches along the southern stretch are mostly shingle, but you will find miles and miles of sandy beach along the north eastern Kent coast stretch.

This bit of the British coast is also quite historically important, and played a major part in our defence during the wars, which you will see on some of the walks.

I've walked a solid chunk of the south east coast, almost all of it. What's left are the bits which don't look very interesting, or the few sections that are logistically challenging. The walks I have chosen to share here are my favourite parts of the coast, and the walks I keep going back to.

One of my favourite things about walking along the coast (apart from the sea and the cliffs), is that you can just switch off completely and not worry too much about navigation.

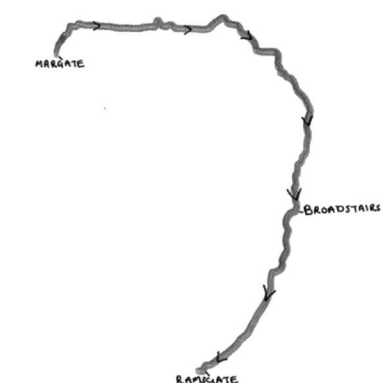

WALK 25

Margate to Ramsgate via Broadstairs

This walk takes you along what I think are the best beaches on the South East coast. The South East coast is predominantly shingle. Not here. This is pure sand goodness. It links three historic towns, Margate, Broadstairs, and Ramsgate on the Isle of Thanet, the far east peninsula of Kent.

What I find interesting is how similar but different each place is. They all have this old world feeling but in their own very unique way.

The whole walk can be done at sea level, on either the under cliff path, sea bed, and beach or alternatively along the clifftop. This is however, determined by the tide, with a lot of the sea level walking only accessible at low tide. I like to walk at sea level. Walking on ground that is under the sea for half of the day is quite interesting, and also spectacular with the cliffs looming above. There is a sort of comforting bleakness to it.

The first time I did this walk, was my first time ever to this part of the coast. Arriving in Margate I felt a sort of nostalgia for my childhood. This was the first time in a long time that I had been somewhere like this. I spent a lot of my childhood in Essex with my grandmother, playing on the beach a few minutes walk from her home. The salty air heavy with English humidity, the smell, the sounds all transported me back to that time. There was a lot of noise, of people talking, kids playing, music coming from different directions. The sky was gloomy, but that never stops the British flocking to the beach in the summer.

You next have a series of beaches. Gorgeous stretches of sandy beaches.

WHAT TO EXPECT

From Margate, it's a short walk to the coast and then onto the under cliff path.

Margate will probably be quite busy, but the craziness should die down a little as you get further away. You next have a series of beaches. Gorgeous stretches of sandy beaches. This is where the tide needs to be out, to get to each route, around the cliff peninsulas. However, if the tide is too high at your time of arrival, it's not too much of an issue as you can go up to the top of the cliff, then back down to each.

You might find the crowds pick up again at some of the beaches, but then it's silence, as you turn the cliff corners.

There is a long stretch of sea bed walking after Joss Bay. The terrain can be a little trickier on this bit, with all the rocks, rock pools, and seaweed.

FUN FACT:

A couple of interesting ones here. Broadstairs was a favourite holiday spot for Charles Dickens, and Ramsgate used to have its own meridian line, 5min 41s ahead of GMT.

You will know you are near Broadstairs (about 6 miles in), when you see all the beach huts, colourful beach huts lining the bottom of the cliff.

Next it's more undercliff path, beaches, and sea bed (this time more sandy, so a bit nicer on the feet) below the big white looming cliffs, as you head to Ramsgate.

From Ramsgate, it's then about a 15/20 min walk to get to the station. Which is annoying. But hey ho.

DIRECTORY

LOGISTICS:

Start/Finish: Margate Station, Ramsgate Station. Kent.
Difficulty: Easy.
Type: Point to point.
Route Distance: 9 miles/14.5 km.
Time: 3–4h.

HOW TO GET THERE:

The quickest route by train is from London St Pancras southern approach. So buy a return ticket to Margate, and get on the train that travels through Ramsgate first. It's the high speed train. Journey time 1h30 min. The return can be used from Ramsgate after the walk. If you don't mind a longer journey, and want a cheaper ticket, you can get direct trains from London Victoria. In this case you'll buy a return ticket to Ramsgate, then get off two stops ealy in Margate to start the walk.

COMING BY CAR:

There are quite a lot of car parks about, in each of the towns and in between. You would then do the walk, and return by train depending on where you choose to start. Trinity Square car park CT9 1LZ in Margate, RingGo App payment. Staffordshire Street Parking CT11 8NT, Albion Place car park CT11 8HQ in Ramsgate, RingGo App payment.

ELEVATION GAIN:

Flat unless you decide to walk up along the clifftop.

TERRAIN:

Sand, rocks, concrete, some road. No stiles.

DOG FRIENDLY:

Sometimes. No dogs allowed on the beaches from 1st May–30th Sept between 10am and 6pm. So you'll either have to walk on the clifftop, or wait until winter-ish.

PHONE SIGNAL:

Mostly yes, but some loss under the cliffs and around Broadstairs.

PUBLIC TOILETS:

Yes, at each of the train stations, and in each of the towns. At Joss Bay, seasonal opening hours, a couple along the clifftop between Broadstairs and Ramsgate.

IDEAL TIME OF YEAR:

Anytime is great. Summer is good if you want to take a dip. Winter is good for less people.

OPTION TO SHORTEN THE WALK:

Yes, at Broadstairs there is a station. All three stations are on the same train line, one stop away from each other, so you can use the same ticket. Margate to Broadstairs is 6 miles. Ramsgate to Broadstairs is 3 miles. If you want the best beaches do Margate to Broadstairs. If you want something short, do Ramsgate to Broadstairs.

WHERE TO EAT?

Tons of options in each of the towns. These are some recommendations.

CAFE AND COFFEE:

Margate

- The Bus Cafe (dogs allowed outside).
- Garage Coffee Roasters (dog friendly).

PUB:

Ramsgate

- Royal Victoria Pavillion (it's a Wetherspoons, but worth a mention as it's significant. It's the largest one in the UK and is in a Grade II listed building/ dogs not allowed).

RESTAURANTS:

Margate

- Buoy and Oyster (dogs not allowed).
- Dory's (dog friendly).

Ramsgate

- Shakey Shakey Fish Bar (dog friendly).
- Royal Harbour Brasserie (dog friendly).

FOR SUPPLIES:

Supermarkets or convenience stores in each of the towns.

TIPS/OTHER THINGS TO KNOW

- The walk is good in either direction. So which way you choose should be determined by what the tide is doing. If it's coming in, start from Ramsgate, as the first sea bed section is close to here. If it's on its way out, but still a bit high, start from Margate. Just Google 'tide times Margate'.
- If you do get caught out by the tide though, that's OK! At each beach there is a way up to the clifftop where you can complete the walk. I would just be careful though at some sections, where there is a longer stretch below the cliffs between the beaches. If the tide is coming in and close, it's best to not risk getting caught out and instead go up to the clifftop.
- If you're up for it, take swimwear and have a dip in the sea. There are plenty of beaches to choose from. About 1 mile into the walk there is a tidal pool and the Haeckels community sauna. It's free to use, and is operated by volunteers, but you can donate via their Facebook Page, which helps with the running costs.
- Be careful below the cliffs. Particularly when walking on the sea bed sections. Don't go too close as they are a little crumbly.
- You can wear trainers for this one.

On the other end of the beach is an impressive rock arch to get you to the next beach.

ROUTE DESCRIPTION

Out of the station, head to the coast, and turn right. There's a sort of retro feel to Margate as you pass by a place called Dreamland, an old amusement park.

Keep following the coast as it takes you around the Turner Gallery (to your right).

Look out to sea and you might see a man statue. This is the Anthony Gormley Another Time statue. Completely underwater at high tide.

Keep going and you'll pass an area with lots of graffiti to reach the under cliff path.

The beaches

The under cliff path will continue for a bit over 1 mile, passing by the Walpole Tidal Pool and the Haeckels community sauna. It's a cute looking thing and was put in place to give back to the local community and encourage people to get out to the beaches in the colder months. The firewood is sustainably sourced and the ash is composted locally to support growth of local produce.

Next you'll reach Palm Bay. A lovely sandy beach. A better one is about to come though.

Around the next peninsula (which is under water at high tide) you will reach Botany Bay. This is my favourite beach. This is a good old long stretch of wonderful sand.

Towards the other end of this beach are these cool rocks. That's also where there are lifeguards if you want to get into the sea but want some safety backup.

Two route options

At this point you have a couple of good options. If you stay down at beach level, around the rocks you will reach a sort of secret bay, which I've heard is an unofficial nudist beach. Then on the other end of the beach is an impressive rock arch to get you to the next beach, Kingsgate Bay. You need the tide to be out to do this though.

Your other option is to head to the clifftop at the end of Botany Bay. Up there you will pass by the ruins of an 18th century folly. It's called Neptune's Tower, and then you will get a cool view down to Kingsgate Bay and to Kingsgate Castle.

Then when you reach the steps down, go back down onto the beach (Kingsgate Bay).

Whichever route you took, you can walk around the castle at beach level. This bit here is cut off at high tide by the way.

Walk to Broadstairs

The next beach is Joss Bay. This is a small one, then around the next bit of cliff is a long stretch of sea bed. This is where you want to be careful if the tide is coming in, as you won't be able to get back up for a bit.

The terrain is a bit tricky. With rocks, rock pools, and seaweed. There is a sort of bleakness to it. I kind of like it. Somewhere around here is also the most eastern point of Kent.

Next you will reach Stone Bay, and all those colourful beach huts, lining the bottom of the cliff, and back to the under cliff path. This path will now lead you up to Broadstairs.

A charming seaside village with an interesting interjection of modern into old world. Narrow lanes, historic architecture, cute cafes, modern restaurants, and a 1950's ice cream parlour.

Walk to Ramsgate

After you have done your thing in Broadstairs, head back down to the beach. This is Viking Bay. You next have a bit of under cliff path before a long stretch that is underwater at high tide. It's nice and sandy, so easy to walk along.

Then you reach the under cliff path again as you head into Ramsgate, with it's Regency and Victorian architecture, and yacht packed marina lending to a more continental vibe. Interestingly, this is England's only Royal Harbour.

From the Marina, you can turn in for that long walk to the station.

Walk 25

Margate to Ramsgate via Broadstairs

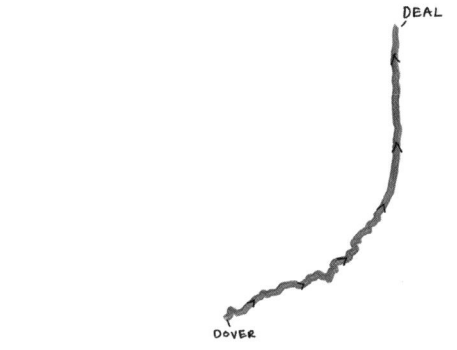

WALK 26

Dover to Deal

This is one of my favourite coastal walks from London, taking you from the major ferry port town of Dover to the former fishing, mining, and garrison town of Deal.

You will see the famous white cliffs of Dover, pass through the small village of Saint Margaret's at Cliffe with its secluded bay, see a few castles, and on a clear day can see France (and your phone might think you are over there too).

Dover is quite an important place. It was once our front defence line during the first and second world wars, and you will see a few war things about. Now it's the busiest international passenger ferry port in the UK.

Dover is also the closest point in England to continental Europe, and is known as the 'Gateway to England'.

*Couple of castles
and beach huts
along the way.*

WHAT TO EXPECT

It's a chunky uphill to get up the clifftop at Dover, where you will be greeted with an ugly view down to the ferry port. However, very soon after, you will get a wonderful view to the Langdon Cliffs ahead, and after a few steep but short undulations, more cliffs behind. The kind of views that make you stop in your tracks.

At around the 3 mile mark, you pass by the South Foreland lighthouse, after which, the trail levels off with gentle undulations.

At around 5 miles, you reach St Margaret's Bay, which you can take a swim in. You do have to walk downhill to get to it though, which means an uphill to get back out.

It's then a long stretch of clifftop trail, fields, and meadows, on a gentle decline, with occasional up, and occasional cliff view. In the summer, this is probably my favourite section of the walk. It's very pretty.

At around the 7.5 mile mark, you descend the cliffs and finish off with a few miles along a seemingly never ending path to reach the charming Deal, passing a couple of castles and beach huts along the way.

FUN FACT:

The Deal pier is the last remaining fully intact leisure pier in Kent and is Grade II listed.

Dover to Deal

DIRECTORY

LOGISTICS:

Start/Finish: Dover Priory Station, Deal Station. Kent.
Difficulty: Moderate.
Type: Point to point.
Route Distance: 11 miles/17.5 km.
Time: 4–5h.

HOW TO GET THERE:

Direct trains run from London St Pancras on the Southeastern High Speed train. Buy a return ticket to Deal which will cover the whole journey. Get off three stops earlier to start in Dover. Journey time is about 1h 5 min.

COMING BY CAR:

You can park in Dover or Deal and get the train back at the end, however, I would personally park somewhere else along the route as the walk from Dover to the cliffs is noisy, and the walk from Deal to the cliffs is never ending. Your options are White Cliffs of Dover car park CT16 1HJ. St Margaret's Bay CT15 6DU. These are paid parking. You would then make this an out and back walk. The exact route depends on where you choose to park. It's easy to navigate though as you're just following the coast path.

ELEVATION GAIN:

427m/1401ft.

TERRAIN:

Grass, dirt, chalk, gravel, steps, concrete, asphalt, shingle. No stiles.

DOG FRIENDLY:

Yes, with restrictions. At St Margaret's Bay they must be on a lead, and are not allowed from 1 May to 30 September. Must be on a lead along some of the clifftop in the National Trust area 1st March–31st August. There are also some loose cows about.

PHONE SIGNAL:

There is phone signal for the majority, however, patches of no signal on the cliffs and your phone will think you are in France around the Dover end.

PUBLIC TOILETS:

Yes. At Dover Priory and Deal stations, the Dover Cliffs National Trust Centre, St Margaret's Bay, and Kingsdown (April–Sept only).

IDEAL TIME OF YEAR:

Summer is my favourite time, as there are a lot of flowers and prettiness, plus it's the perfect time for taking a dip at St Margaret's Bay.

OPTION TO SHORTEN THE WALK:

Only if you walk out and back. How far you go is up to you. An idea would be Dover to South Foreland Lighthouse, this is 8 miles out and back.

WHERE TO EAT?

A number of options along the route, then plenty to choose from in Dover and Deal. These are some recommendations.

CAFE AND COFFEE:

On the walk

- 4 miles: Mrs Knott's Tea Room, South Foreland Lighthouse (dogs allowed outside).
- 5 miles: Margaret's Bay riverside snacks hut (dog friendly).

Deal

- Middle Street Coffee (dog friendly).

PUB:

On the walk

- 5 miles: The Coast Guard pub, St Margaret's Bay (dog friendly).
- 8 miles: Zeltland Arms Pub, Kingsdown (dog friendly).

Deal

- Kings Head (dog friendly).

FOR SUPPLIES:

Supermarkets in both Dover and Deal.

TIPS/OTHER THINGS TO KNOW

- The Dover Cliffs end can get very busy, but the crowds tend to die down once you pass the South Foreland Lighthouse. I would however avoid public holidays, and if you are doing this on a summer weekend, start very early to get ahead of the crowds.
- It can be walked in both directions, but I prefer this way, as Deal is a much nicer place to finish.
- Take swimwear/towel if you fancy a dip at St Margaret's Bay.
- Although I always advise hiking boots, you could probably get away with trainers if you must, most of the terrain is easy, and I've walked this in all seasons and never encountered too much mud (don't come at me if you find yourself in mud).

Seeing that really does make the uphill worth it.

ROUTE DESCRIPTION

From Dover Priory Station, it's about a 15 min walk to get to the cliffs, and just to warn you, it isn't the nicest walk.

So turn left out of the station onto the main road, then at the roundabout, over to the left is a pedestrian crossing. Cross over, then turn right to walk past the roundabout and then take any of the next few left turns. This will lead you to Biggin Street where you turn right.

You can follow this now, past the market square, then down the underpass to reach the seafront. There are a few coffee shops along this bit if you need a last minute boost. When you reach the seafront, turn left to walk towards the big white cliffs ahead. You will need to walk up that soon, and yes, it will feel like it looks.

As you near the end of the promenade, there is a traffic light crossing with a trail signpost. Cross the road, then walk along the road behind the houses you will see in front. It's a surprise road with colourful house facades. Keep going past the houses, to reach a barrier, which looks like a no entry barrier, but it's not.

Go through it, then you will start to make your way up the hill. There are some steps, some bushy bits, and you will walk under a noisy road bridge. Then as you get higher, look to the left and you will have a nice view to Dover Castle.

At the top, the entrance to the National Trust Dover Cliffs is straight ahead.

Follow the road through, past the car park and the National Trust Cafe, with a view down to the right of the port with big ferries.

Stay on this road to the end, and you will reach a gate.

Walk over the Langdon cliffs

Through the gate, you will reach a fork in the path. Take the left to walk gently uphill on an immaculate path. Then through the gate at the top, you will get your first breathtaking view of the Langdon Cliffs ahead.

Seeing that really does make the uphill worth it.

You will notice people walking below, and you can see various trails across the undulating grassy clifftop ahead. These are all optional, so feel free to wander. I'm going to show you the main route through though.

If you are looking for the best cliff views, this spot here (or the ledge below) is one of them. The next one comes a bit later.

The immaculate path now turns into a narrow dirt track, and then neat gravel, as it takes you along the undulating clifftop. There are a few steep bits to begin with, but it will then level out somewhat. Stay on the main trail, as it loops you around, then when you reach the other side, you get that other fantastic cliff view I mentioned earlier.

Walk to South Foreland Lighthouse

Further along this neat, well kept trail, when you walk around the next big dip in the cliffs, make sure to look back to see the South Foreland sound mirror nestled in the side of the hill. These were used during the war to hear enemy aircraft approaching.

It wasn't until maybe the fourth time I walked this route that I noticed it.

Keep going, and you will next reach a gate with the South Foreland Lighthouse ahead. Don't go through the gate, instead, follow the trail to the right of it. This will lead you to a different gate.

Go through this one, then take either of the two trails ahead, to walk up the hill then follow the hedge around the right side of the lighthouse to reach a gate.

Through this one you will be on a narrow trail, to reach an entrance gate to the lighthouse. You can go in if you wish, however, to continue on the walk, turn right here, then at the end, turn right onto the track.

FUN FACT:

Theres a lovely 1950's themed tea room at the lighthouse. Although, even more interesting is the cabin hut book nook. It's a nice place to go for shelter if the weather is questionable (I've taken shelter in there). With historical relics, cosy seating, and books you can purchase with a donation.

Walk to St Margaret's Bay

If the trail has been a bit congested with other people, then it should die down around here.

Continue on for about 500m, then you should see a trail turning on the right. Follow this, then at the grass trail junction, you can take either, but I'd suggest taking the right one. This will lead you around then down the grass clifftop with a wonderful view to the white cliffs ahead. That's St Margaret's Bay down there.

Keep going all the way to the end, then through the gate you will reach a rugged road. Walk down it, then at the junction, turn right onto the proper road. You are now in St Margaret's at Cliffe.

Walk down to the other end of the road, then turn right, and at the fork just ahead, take the right again. This will lead you down to the beach, surrounded by the impressive white cliffs.

There used to be another route down, avoiding some of the road. It involved steep shallow steps that you had to walk sideways down to fit your feet on. It's now closed off for safety reasons. I miss it.

I like to sit on the far right side of this shingle beach. It's away from the car park, and most people. If you look at the cliff to the right, you will see a structure nestled in it. I have no idea what this is, but I always wonder when I am there.

Walk to Kingsdown

To get out of St Margaret's Bay, walk to the east (or the left from the way you entered), and look out for a trail sign pointing into a gap. This will lead you up some steps. Actually, lots of steps.

But good news, this is the last big uphill of the walk.

After the steps, it's uphill through woods, then out in the open and uphill some more. When you get up there, make sure to look back for a wonderful view back to the bay. There is a section coming up along a narrow dirt trail through scratchy bushes, still uphill.

Once you are out of it, the landscape opens up with a view to clifftop fields spreading out as far as the eye can see. It's all easy now. Going forward, the views are less cliffy, and more English countryside. There is the occasional peak of white cliff, but mostly not. This section is wonderful in the summer, with all the flowers, and incredibly peaceful all year around. You will be on a gentle decline, with occasional up, as you make your way across the fields.

Just before the descent down to Kingsdown, there is a car park. Keep to the trail on the right side of it, and a view down to the beach at Kingsdown will open up ahead.

Through some bushes, you will reach the steps to get down to it.

FUN FACT:
In 1926, the first woman to swim the English Channel made landfall at Kingsdown. Her name is Gertrude Ederle, and she was 19 at the time.

Walk to Deal

You have a choice now of shingle or road. This bit is the only time I recommend the shingle, as you are about to have a very long stretch on hard ground.

The shingle doesn't go on for too long though, to get you onto the promenade.

The promenade is short, and before the end, you need to take the obvious left opening, past the beach huts, to reach the trail alongside the houses.

From here, just keep going straight and you will (eventually) reach Deal. First though, you will pass by Walmer Castle, and a long stretch of memorial benches, then Deal Castle. There is a shingle beach to the right, but you probably won't want to walk on that.

I always find this stretch of the walk the toughest. There isn't much in the way of views, and the ground is hard. The first time I did this walk I actually had headwinds, which made it more relentless.

Arriving in Deal though, is like the light at the end of the tunnel. A charming traditional seaside town, with a buzzing pub with a beer garden overlooking the ocean, a pier, and the smell of fish and chips. Very British.

WALK 27

Seven Sisters Cliffs: Seaford to Eastbourne

The Seven Sisters Cliffs walk is probably one of the most well known walks that you can do as a day trip from London, and it's not hard to see why.

I have done this walk countless times and the magnificent white chalk cliff views always take my breath away.

Located in the South Downs National Park, and part of the South Downs Way National Trail, each sister represents a hill, although you will walk up and down a lot more than that. Basically it's a very hilly walk. Although, the scenery is so jaw dropping that you hardly notice all the hills. Actually, you definitely notice, but somehow the beauty takes the edge off.

You can do the walk in either direction, but I think the views are a bit better this way. That's not to say the other direction is bad, it's just a slightly lower level of amazing.

*As long as you
keep the sea to your right,
you're good.*

WHAT TO EXPECT

Almost immediately you are faced with your first big hill. This is Seaford head. A warm up for the others. As you descend this hill on the other side, you will have a view of the Seven Sisters ahead of you.

To get to them involves a bit of a detour. The Cuckmere River is in the way. There was a time many years ago, where at low tide the river vanished. It doesn't do this anymore. So now you'll need to walk about 2 miles along the river and back to reach the cliffs.

Once on the sisters, you undulate across them. Up, down, up, down, to reach Birling Gap. It's all grass up top, and is a very large area. The Birling Gap area will be quite busy. The area is owned by the National Trust, with all the tourist things that go with it.

It is also the end of the Seven Sisters Cliffs, but it's not the end of the walk. You have more cliff to walk across, and more hills, although not as aggressive.

FUN FACT:

The Seven Sisters Cliffs are often used in filming locations as a stand in for the famous White Cliffs of Dover as they are free of any modern development. Also, Cuckmere Haven has been used as a filming location for a number of shows and movies inducing Robin Hood and Atonement.

Next you reach the Beachy Head Lighthouse viewpoint, and then you reach a bushy area with many trails to choose from, to reach Eastbourne. You can freestyle here. As long as you keep the sea to your right, you're good.

Once you reach Eastbourne, it's a solid 30min walk to actually reach the train station. You can walk most of the way on the seafront though, so it's not too bad.

DIRECTORY

LOGISTICS:

Start/Finish: Seaford Station, Eastbourne Station. East Sussex.
Difficulty: Moderate/Challenging.
Type: Point to point.
Route Distance: 13.5 miles/21.5 km.
Time: 4–5h.

HOW TO GET THERE:

From London to Seaford and Eastbourne, the train follows the same line up until Lewes. This train will continue on to Eastbourne, but you will need to change at Lewes to reach Seaford. So, buy a return ticket from London Victoria to Eastbourne, and a single ticket from Lewes to Seaford. Journey time is about 1h 25min. You can then use your return ticket to come back to London at the end.

COMING BY CAR:

Car parking at Seaford Richmond Road car park BN25 1DB or West Street car park BN25 1EE (and then you can follow my route description). Or Exceat BN25 1QL, Birling Gap BN20 0AD, Beachy Head BN20 7YA, and Eastbourne Wish Tower car park BN21 4DR. All pay parking. There are then buses along the route. See route description for how to modify the route.

ELEVATION GAIN:

532m/1745ft.

TERRAIN:

Grass, dirt trails, shingle. No stiles.

DOG FRIENDLY:

As long as they are safe with the cliff edge. There can be some loose sheep about. I've only ever seen them at the Beachy Head end though. There isn't much shelter either.

PHONE SIGNAL:

Yes.

PUBLIC TOILETS:

Public toilets at both stations, and at Exceat, Birling Gap, and Beachy Head.

IDEAL TIME OF YEAR:

Any time of year is great, I would just avoid extremes of weather though, as it's quite exposed.

OPTION TO SHORTEN THE WALK:

Yes, there are a number of ways, which I have detailed at the relevant points in the route description.

WHERE TO EAT?
CAFE AND COFFEE:

Seaford

- Baca's Coffee Bar

On the walk

- 4 miles: The Saltmarsh and Farmhouse Cafe (dog friendly).
- 7.5 miles: The National Trust Cafe at Birling Gap (dogs only allowed outside).
- 10 miles: The Cadence Cycle Club Cafe,
- Beachy Head (dog friendly).

PUB:

Seaford

- The Steamworks (dog friendly).

On the walk

- 4 miles: The Cuckmere Inn (dog friendly).

Eastbourne

- The Pilot Inn (dog friendly).

FOR SUPPLIES:

Morrisons in Seaford, multiple supermarkets in Eastbourne.

TIPS/OTHER THINGS TO KNOW

- Wear high factor sunscreen, even if it's overcast. The worst burns I have ever got were on this hike, on an overcast day, and I was wearing sunscreen.
- In the morning, the sun will be ahead of you, in the afternoon it will be behind. So if you start early on a sunny day, you might want sunglasses or a hat.
- Don't go close to the edge. The cliffs are very unstable. If you look closely, you can actually see cracks in the cliffs where they are at risk of falling.
- Also, be careful if you choose to go down to beach level and walk under the cliffs, as you will be at risk of falling rocks.
- Hiking boots recommended.
- If you want to shorten the walk and catch a bus, the 12X bus runs from Seaford to Eastbourne via Exceat Monday–Saturday. 13X bus runs from Seaford to Eastbourne via Exceat, Birling Gap and Beachy Head on Sunday. Check timetables before heading out, particularly the Sunday service, as it's limited.

*It's a nice detour,
and does make for an
interesting change in scenery*

ROUTE DESCRIPTION

Once out of the station, take a right and head to the sea. It's only a 5min walk. You will pass a supermarket, giving you a chance to get any supplies you may have forgotten. Once you reach the shingle beach, take a left, and you will get your first grand white cliffs view. Seaford Head.

Now head towards these cliffs. From here on out you will be walking with the sea to your right for the whole way. Seaford Head will be your first uphill, and as you reach the top you get great views back over Seaford.

Next you will walk past a golf course, before getting your first glimpse of the magnificent Seven Sisters Cliffs ahead. The valley below it is Cuckmere Haven. Head towards it.

Cuckmere Haven

Cuckmere Haven is where the South Downs meets the sea. This is where the Seven Sisters Cliffs start. But first off you need to navigate the Cuckmere River.

Option to shorten the walk: If you'd like to stop here, then walk back to Seaford, it's roughly 6 miles.

FUN FACT:

This area was very popular for smugglers between the 16th and 18th centuries. At low tide, you can also see part of a German shipwreck. There is an opportunity for a dip in the sea here. I actually find it more pleasant to get in when the tide is high. Less big rocks in the way.

To continue on, follow the river towards Exceat, then cross the bridge and follow it back. It's a nice detour, and does make for an interesting change in scenery.

Option to shorten the walk: You can stop/start the walk from Exceat as there are buses. To walk from Seaford to Exceat is roughly 4 miles. To walk from Exceat and over the Seven Sisters to Birling gap is roughly 3 miles, where you can catch the bus (Sundays only).

Walk across the Seven Sisters

As you head up the first sister, it is quite steep and could be slippy if your shoes don't have good grip.

At the top, take a look back for a great view back over the beach and the Cuckmere Valley. This is also where the trail becomes part of the South Downs Way.

Now make your way across them. It's up and down for some time now. About 2.5 miles, but it feels a lot longer. There is the occasional bit of trail, but it's mostly just grass. It can be easy to find yourself close to the edge, so be careful.

Walk to Birling Gap

As you are coming down off the last sister, the trail will lead you to a road. Turn right, and follow it down to reach Birling Gap. This marks the end of the sisters.

If you'd like to freshen up, there are toilets and a cafe here. You can also visit the tourist centre, or have some beach time and take a dip in the sea.

If you want to escape the crowds, just continue past along the cliffs. Most people visiting Birling Gap will stay in the area of the cliffs either side.

You have the option to stop or start the walk from here. There is a car park and bus links on Sundays.

If you prefer to start the walk from Eastbourne, it's roughly 6 miles to get here from Eastbourne Station or, starting from Birling Gap, it's a bit over 5 miles to walk the length of the Sevens Sisters and back.

Walk to Belle Tout lighthouse

Up the next hill, you will reach the Belle Tout Lighthouse, which has had an interesting life. It was built in the early 1800's, however, its location meant that it was frequently covered by the clifftop fog. So it wasn't very good at doing its job of warning passing ships. As such, it was decommissioned in the early 1900's. It then became a family home and tea house, which was almost destroyed during WWII, then got bought by the BBC as a filming location.

Due to the cliff erosion it was in danger of falling into the sea, and in 1999 was moved back 17 meters from the cliff edge. It now has new owners who have converted it into a bed and breakfast. It's my dream to one day stay there.

Past the Belle Tout Lighthouse, you will get that iconic view to Beachy Head Lighthouse.

Walk to Beachy Head

It's downhill now towards the cute candy cane coloured Beachy Head Lighthouse. It seems rather tiny in comparison to the looming white cliffs. It was built in the early 1900's to take over lighthouse duties of the Belle Tout Lighthouse.

You then have your last big uphill, up Beachy Head. At 162m above sea level, it is the highest chalk sea cliff in Britain.

Beachy Head is the stuff of poetry, I mean that literally. Many poems have been written about it. The area has also featured in film and television including Harry Potter, James Bond and Black Mirror.

Walk to Eastbourne

Past Beachy Head, the landscape changes, featuring a lot more flora and fauna. During summer it's all bright pinks and purples.

There are multiple trail options to get to Eastbourne, so you can freestyle a bit here. Just as long as you keep heading in the same direction, with the sea to your right. And the more right you go, the hillier it will be. So if you are fed up with the hills, then keep a bit more to the left.

I would recommend keeping to the right trail though, along the coastal path, as you'll go past another nice viewpoint for the lighthouse along here.

As you reach the end of the South Downs National Park, it's a short downhill, then once you reach the bottom, there is still a few miles of walking to go to get to the station.

I would suggest walking along the seafront. There are actually two different paths here. One along the promenade, and one slightly higher up lined with bushes and trees, which is very pretty.

To get to the station, make sure to turn in just before you reach the pier.

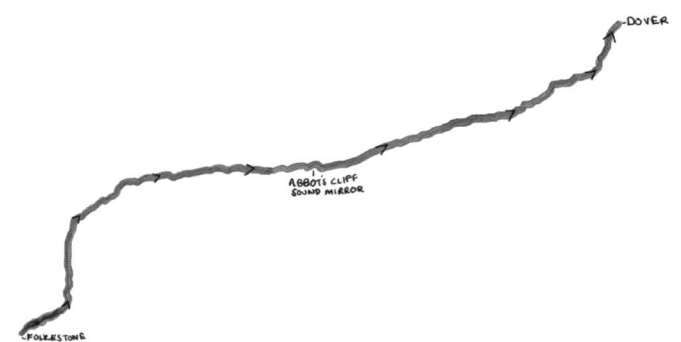

WALK 28

Folkestone to Dover

This is a nice little walk, taking you between a small arty port town and a major industrial vibes port town, with cliffs in between. I like to come and do this walk if I need something simple to follow, that's not too long, and gives me some cliff goodness.

There is a lot of history along this one, with Dover being a frontline town, protecting Britain from invasion. Roman Forts, Napoleonic forts, and defence systems from the World Wars.

There is one particularly fun bit where you are walking along a cliffside trail.

WHAT TO EXPECT

The walk starts out along the seafront in Folkestone, as you head towards the cliffs ahead, passing by various arty things. Then it's a very steep and long uphill to reach the clifftop, after which, it's pretty flat for around the next 4ish miles (with one hill thrown in). You'll have cliffy and coastline views in both directions, and a cool view down to the railway, pass by the Battle of Britain Memorial, a sound mirror, pillboxes and forts.

A lot of the walk is close to the edge, but I've never really felt concerned of falling, and there is one particularly fun bit where you are walking along a cliffside trail. As in, on the side of the cliff.

As you approach Dover, there are some sneaky hills, and you will be able to see the ships coming in, in the distance. Then there is one last fun thing before you finish. Instead of walking down to the seafront, you will turn in to walk through Western Heights, through a tiny tunnel where you will need to crouch down, and then around an impressive fort, with views of Dover Castle. And from there, it's a short walk to the station.

Now, one thing to be aware of, is there is a big aggressive road which follows the trail from about halfway. You will hear it. How much you hear it really depends on the wind direction, and how many cars are out that day. I've had times where I barely notice it until near the end, and other times it's quite loud for a few miles.

FUN FACT:
You will walk past the Abbot's Cliff Sound Mirror. This was used during the war to hear enemy aircraft, before we had more advanced radar systems. How it works is that it reflects sound waves. There are a bunch of them along the south coast.

DIRECTORY

LOGISTICS:

Start/Finish: Folkestone Central Station, Dover Priory Station, Kent.
Difficulty: Moderate.
Type: Point to point.
Route Distance: 9 miles/14.5 km.
Time: 3–4h.

HOW TO GET THERE:

Buy a return ticket from London St Pancras to Dover Priory for the Southeastern High Speed train, then get off one stop early in Folkestone. Journey time 55min.

COMING BY CAR:

You can park at Folkestone Harbour CT20 1QH, or Albany Place car park Dover CT17 9AS. Both pay parking.

ELEVATION GAIN:

426m/1398ft.

TERRAIN:

Grass, dirt trail, road, steps. No stiles.

DOG FRIENDLY:

Somewhat. Be wary of the cliff edges. There are some narrow bits with steep drops. On a lead around the Battle of Britain Memorial. I've never seen livestock, but I've heard they are sometimes about.

PHONE SIGNAL:

Yes.

PUBLIC TOILETS:

Yes, at both stations, or if you visit the Battle of Britain Memorial.

IDEAL TIME OF YEAR:

Anytime of year is good, avoiding weather extremes as it's an exposed walk. I personally prefer overcast and moody.

OPTION TO SHORTEN THE WALK:

Yes. The 102 bus runs along part of the route and goes to Dover and Folkestone. It runs along New Dover Road and you can catch it at the Battle of Britain Memorial (roughly 2.5 miles from Folkestone), or outside the Royal Oak pub (4ish miles from Folkestone).

WHERE TO EAT?
CAFE AND COFFEE:

Folkstone

- Steep Street Coffee House (dog friendly).

On the walk

- 2.5 miles: Cockpit Cafe, at the Battle of Britain Memorial (dogs not allowed).
- 3 miles: The Clifftop Cafe (dog friendly).

PUB:

Folkstone

- The Harbour Inn (dog friendly).

On the walk

- 4 miles: The Royal Oak Pub (this one is slightly off trail/ dog friendly).

Dover

- The White Horse (dog friendly).

FOR SUPPLIES:

A number of supermarkets in both Folkstone and Dover.

TIPS/OTHER THINGS TO KNOW

- It can be walked in either direction, but having done both ways, I prefer this way due to the variety in the views ahead. If walking the other way, you have pretty much the same view for half the walk. However, Folkstone is a much nicer place to finish, with better food options, so if this is more important to you, walk the other direction. Also, if you'd rather get the road nonsense out of the way first, then start from Dover.

- Wear sunscreen, even if it's overcast. That's when the sun gets you.

- For the road noise, a northerly wind will make it sound louder. Southerly wind will make it quieter.

- Dover can be a bit of a shock to the system, which is why this guide doesn't take you to the seafront. The road to walk there is nasty. It's big and loud, and goes on for longer than is desirable.

- Hiking boots recommended.

Walk through the Warren. This way is more wild.

ROUTE DESCRIPTION

Out of the station, it's about a 10min walk to get to the seafront. First turn right, then walk along Cheriton Road past the Co-op. At the main road, turn left which is still Cheriton Road. At the end, which is an even bigger road, turn left, and cross over at the pedestrian crossing.

Now this is where it can get confusing. I recommend walking along the Old High Street. It's a narrow pedestrian only street full of cafes, galleries, and independent shops, all with colourful facades.

To get there, continue now along Guildhall Street, which then becomes Rendezvous Street. Keep on this road as it curves left, and it will lead you to the Old High Street where you turn right. Then take the first left which is the continuation of the Old High Street. This will lead you to the seafront. If in doubt, Google Maps this bit.

When you reach the seafront, turn left and follow it along, under the bridge, and past the boats in the harbour. Look out for the floating pink house. This is a cartoon style model holiday home created by the artist Richard Woods. Apparently there are six of these dotted around Folkestone. He created them for the Folkestone Triennial Festival in 2017, in response to the housing crisis and boom in second homes.

Walk all the way to the other end of the promenade, around Folkestone Beach, and then up the steps. These are to warm up your legs for the big uphill coming soon.

Up the steps, head up the little hill in front, to reach the green, and turn right, to walk toward the big yellow horn. This was also commissioned for the Triennial Festival in 2017, this time by Marc Schmitz and Dolgor Ser-Od. Sort of a play on the sound mirrors (which you will see later). It amplifies the sounds of the waves, like a seashell. It is also a reminder of the fog horn that used to sound from the lighthouse.

The golf course or the Warren

Past the horn, go through the gate, and you now have two route options.

Option 1. Walk through the golf course. You should see a way up to the golf course on the left. Then follow the right perimeter all the way around, and out the other end onto the green next to the road. You will get a nice view over the rooftops of Folkestone going this way.

Option 2. Walk through the Warren. This way is more wild. Stay on this path and it will lead you to the rugged trail, winding through the close bushes. Out the other end, you will reach that green. There are some junctions before you reach the green, but stay on this main path.

You will see a big cliff ahead at this point. That's where you are heading to. Up the top. Yes, it is as aggressively high and tough as it looks.

You should also be able to see a Martello Tower ahead. There are a bunch of these dotted along the England coastline. They are defensive forts built to protect against invasion from Napoleon's French army.

Walk to the other end of the green, then turn right to walk up the road. A short way up, where the road bends, you should see a trail leading off it straight ahead. Go up that.

This is the big one.

It's now a chunky uphill walk to get to the clifftop. You will get hot, sweaty, and out of breath.

Walk along the clifftop

Up the top, turn right. You will now be following the North Downs Way to reach Dover. So if you get confused, just follow the signs.

From here, you have a good 4 miles of mostly flat (with some small hills).

It starts off along a narrow trail lined with bushes, then you will enter the large immaculate green that is the site of the Battle of Britain Memorial.

You can have an explore around here, but to continue with the trail, follow the perimeter around, to get back onto the cliff trail.

Soon after you will reach the big dip. Where you go down some steps, then back up the other side through a mass of bushes and trees. This is the only steep bit up here.

Out the other end, you will reach the road. Turn left, then pick up the trail on the right, up a few steps, then along the edge of some peoples' gardens. The trail will guide you back to the cliffs.

It's now more cliff edge walking, with more amazing views to reach a green with wooden benches if you need a break, or, just past here is the Cliff Top Cafe. It can be a little confusing now, the trail runs along the side of the hedges next to the cafe, but you can take the road if you wish, to reach the cliff edge again.

Next it's a series of cliff edge, bushes, another green with benches and views, and a holiday park, to reach the curvy cliffside trail. The fun part.

It's a trail that runs along the side of the cliff, with railings so you don't fall. You also get the best view of the railway below from this spot. You will then reach a small road which leads you to the Abbot's Cliff Sound Mirror.

Continue past the mirror, up the road, and you will reach a gate. Don't go through this one. Over to the right is a smaller gate. Either go through there, or there is a trail to the right. The right trail is closer to the cliff edge though.

I've always taken the trail through the gate, but one time accidentally took the trail closer to the edge. It is very close at points, but you get to see a few things, like a cliffside structure, which I'm going to say is a pillbox, but I'm not 100% certain. You also get a peak to the beaches below.

For the next stretch you are less on cliffside, and more through fields with overgrown grass, and a few bushy bits.

You are now approaching Dover, and history really starts to ramp up, with more war stuff. You'll see various pillboxes including a Dover Quad (which is a type of pillbox). It also means the hills are coming back, and you will start to see them appear ahead of you. Including Shakespeare Cliff, which apparently inspired, you guessed it, Shakespeare. You should also be able to see the big ferries coming into port. Oh and that noisy road I mentioned earlier. It's properly visible now.

Now make your way up and down the hills, keeping the fence just to your right, and then you will be led down a trail to reach the big road underpass.

Walk to Western Heights

Go down the steps and under the underpass, then cross over the road to enter the residential area, where you turn right. You should be on the road called Kings Ropewalk. There are a few twists and turns going forward, but it's signposted with the North Downs Way if you aren't sure.

Follow the road, then after it curves to the left, go up the steps, then turn right through the gate. There is an interesting sitting bench just here.

Keep following this trail up the hill, through a gate, then uphill some more (sorry), to reach the road, where you turn right.

Along the road, you will pass the ruins (or rather base) of a church for the Knights Templar. Keep following the road, and stay straight when it connects to another road.

When you reach the end, turn left, then cross over to take the first right turning onto 'Drop Redoubt' road.

When you reach the fork, take the left, and a short way along, look out for the tunnel to the left. There is a door at the opening.

Now, walk (or crawl) through the tunnel, and you will reach the Drop Redoubt Fort. It's very interesting. You can explore around here, but to continue on, walk around the fort to the right, to reach the opening on the right side, there is a trail. Follow that, and it will lead you around, and up some steps.

Go through a gate, then stay on the trail, and take the first right trail a short way along. Not the steps, the trail! This will lead you along the side of the hill, with some great views over to Dover Castle and down to the port.

When you reach the steps go down them (they are quite steep by the way), then turn right on the road.

Not too far along will be steps to the left, go down them, then turn left, and Dover Priory Station will be just ahead on the right.

WALK 29

Newhaven to Brighton

This walk follows the coast sometimes on the clifftop, sometimes the undercliff path giving you a chance to see the cliffs from different perspectives. Despite being cliffy, it's not too hilly. Apart from the start to get up to the cliffs (and again if you move between the clifftop and undercliff path), it's a gently undulating kind of trail.

If you want a challenge like the Seven Sisters, then this walk isn't the one. But if you want a nice day out, with sea and village views, then this will do nicely.

You could also throw in a bit of a sea swim. Cool off the tired feet.

It's quite cool down there, with the big white cliffs looming above.

WHAT TO EXPECT

It's a bit of a walk to get to the coast from the station, along the river and marina, then you have a hill to get up to the clifftop. Up here you get a really great view to the cliff of Seaford Head in the distance. This is the only big hill, as you now gently undulate along the grass clifftop.

You are never very far from civilisation, passing by one village after another, with a view across the rooftops.

You can walk all the way to Brighton up here, or mix it up with the undercliff path. You reach the first one after about 1.5 miles, which you need to go down some steps to get onto. It's quite cool down there, with the big white cliffs looming above. This path doesn't lead all the way to Brighton, there is a different one for that, so you will need to go back up to the clifftop at some point.

FUN FACT:

The steps you will walk down to get to the undercliff path were in Mr Bean. He walks down them in the episode 'Mr Bean goes to town'.

Once up there, you will now be walking with a road nearby, and the road noises that go with it. It's not the nicest, but you will soon reach the second undercliff path which you can follow all the way to Brighton. It's a lot of hard ground walking on this one, which can be tough on the feet, so think about your footwear wisely.

DIRECTORY

LOGISTICS:

Start/Finish: Newhaven Town Station, Brighton Station. East Sussex.
Difficulty: Easy route, or moderate due to length.
Type: Point to point.
Route Distance: 11.5 miles/18.5 km.
Time: 5h.

HOW TO GET THERE:

There are indirect trains from London Bridge, St Pancras, or Blackfriars (Thameslink with a change at Brighton) and London Victoria (Southern with a change at Lewes) to Newhaven. The London Victoria route is much quicker. From Brighton there are direct trains back to London Bridge, Blackfriars, St Pancras and London Victoria. Journey time is about 1h.

If starting from London Bridge, a return ticket to Newhaven will cover your return from Brighton. If starting from London Victoria, buy a return ticket to Newhaven, then for the way back get a single from Brighton to Haywards Heath, and then your return will cover the remainder of the journey back to London.

COMING BY CAR:

There is a train linking Newhaven and Brighton, journey time 30-ish min. So you can park at either end then get the train back. Free car parking at the clifftop in Newhaven BN9 9DU. If there are no spaces, there are a number of other car parks around Newhaven. Along the route there is free parking at Bastion Steps BN10 8LS.

ELEVATION GAIN:

233m/764ft.

TERRAIN:

Grass, road, undercliff path, steps. No stiles.

DOG FRIENDLY:

Must be on a lead along the Brighton Promenade, and with caution on the clifftops.

PHONE SIGNAL:

Up the top, yes, patchy on some parts under the cliffs.

PUBLIC TOILETS:

Yes. At both train stations, and at Saltdean, Rottingdean, and Ovingdean.

IDEAL TIME OF YEAR:

I would personally avoid really hot summer sunny days for two reasons. The white cliffs will reflect the heat back on to you, and it will be very insanely busy near the Brighton end.

OPTION TO SHORTEN THE WALK:

Yes. At Peacehaven (the first undercliff path) at about 2.5 miles, if you head to the main road, you can catch the 12 coaster bus which takes you to both Brighton and Newhaven. This road follows the rest of the route, so at any point from there you can catch the bus if you are tired.

WHERE TO EAT?

Plenty of opportunities for refreshments in Newhaven, Brighton, and along the route. Here are a few suggestions, but there are lots more.

CAFE AND COFFEE:

Newhaven
- Siding Bistro (dog friendly).

On the walk
- 5 miles: Whitecliffs Cafe, Saltdean (dog friendly).
- 6 miles: Sea Spray Cafe, Rottingdean (dog friendly).
- Daisy's Pantry Artisan Bakery Cafe, Rottingdean (dog friendly).
- 8 miles: Laughing Dog Cafe, Brighton Marina (dog friendly).

PUB:

Newhaven
- The Hope Inn (dog friendly).

On the walk
- 8 miles: The Master Mariner, Brighton marina (dog friendly).

FOR SUPPLIES:

Morrisons in Newhaven. Plenty of places in Brighton.

TIPS/OTHER THINGS TO KNOW

- If you will be walking on all of the undercliff path, you might be more comfortable in trainers. In total, there is about 4 miles on this path which is hard ground. That, on top of walking through Brighton and walking to the cliffs at the start, it will be about 8 miles on hard ground in total.
- With walking under the bright white cliffs, I'd wear sunscreen even if it's overcast. Also take sunnies, I've even burnt under them in November.
- Be careful under the cliffs as they are not that stable, so don't go right next to them.
- Brighton is a very popular place, and you will start to notice the crowds picking up around the second undercliff path.
- My favourite part of the walk is the clifftop from Newhaven to and along the first undercliff path. So if coming by car, I would recommend parking at either the Bastion Steps or Newhaven clifftop car park and walking that stretch and back. That will be about 5 miles.
- The places to eat I have listed, are along the route, however, when you reach Brighton, if you head to The Lanes, you will find tonnes of great options.

*Down here
you get the
full cliff show.*

ROUTE DESCRIPTION

It's about 1.3 miles to get to the clifftop from the station. Turn left out of the station to walk over the bridge then left to follow the River Ouse. At the end, walk around the marina, towards the big green hill you will see ahead.

Past the marina, you should reach a road leading uphill, off this main road. Go up that.

It's a big uphill climb now. Keep going up, around the road bend, and through a car park. You will have a nice view down to Newhaven from up here.

Past the car park, turn to the left to walk up a little more, then look out for a gap in the bushes with a trail sign. Go through there and this will lead you to the clifftop edge, with the coast guard tower to your right and a view to Seaford Beach and Seaford Head to the left.

From here, turn right and follow the clifftop. You will pass by a couple of forts, and have a view over the rooftops of clusters of houses. There aren't a lot of cliffy views at the moment, that will come soon.

The first undercliff path

After about 1.5 miles along the undulating grassy clifftop, you will get a nice view to some cliffs ahead with the undercliff path below them. That's where you are heading.

Just before some houses you will reach the Friers Bay steps, carved into the cliffs, to get you down to the undercliff path. The Mr Bean steps.

Down here you get the full cliff show. The big white cliffs looming above. It's interesting because you mustn't get too close in case rocks fall on you (and there are signs warning of that), but equally there isn't loads of space to keep away.

You can walk for just over 1 mile down here, and then need to go back up. There are two ways up, the first is the Bastion Steps, and the second is more of a slipway type road path near the end.

FUN FACT:
The area is a local geological site and you can spot some giant ammonites.

Back up to the clifftop

Back up top, it's more grass, this time a bit closer to the houses and the road. This is Peacehaven. You will be able to see Brighton in the distance. Well, what you can see is the Brighton Marina area. The station is still a few miles past that.

After a bit over 1/2 a mile, the trail will guide you away from the cliffs for a moment and very close to a noisy road.

Follow the trail around, and over the tarmac, and back onto a green. At the other end of the green, before you go through the gate, take a look back for a nice view back to the cliffs.

Although you are back on the cliff edge, the road noise is still there, but don't worry, it's just a bit over 1/2 a mile until you reach the next undercliff path at Saltdean. You will get a nice view of it ahead as you approach.

The Brighton undercliff path

When you reach Saltdean, make your way to the undercliff path. It's a nice gentle approach this time, not steep steps like the last. You now have 3 miles on this path to reach Brighton.

Along this path, there are two opportunities to get back up top before Brighton. The first time, a bit over 1/2 a mile at Rottingdean, and the second time about 1/2 a mile past that at Ovingdean. So if you want to go up top, make sure to take one of these, otherwise you will be stuck down here until the end.

I would recommend staying down here though, as you will be walking close to the road up the top. Down here it's nice and peaceful.

Brighton

When you reach the black gates, walk through them to enter the Brighton Marina area. It's a nice change from the rest of the path, which I find can start to become a bit samey.

Past the marina, things start to feel a bit more industrial as you pass a big Asda.

It's now about 1.5 miles to reach Brighton Pier.

Before you reach the overhead bridge, turn left to walk along the edge of the Asda car park, and then through the tunnel under the bridge. This will lead you along the seafront. I find this part of the walk a little tedious, as it's usually very busy, and for most of it you will be walking next to a road.

Once you reach Brighton Pier, head into town, and it's just under 1 mile to reach the station. You should also have a wander around the Lanes. It's the historic quarter with winding streets, and where you will find some of the best places to eat.

WALK 30

Herne Bay to Margate

The first time I heard about this walk was many years ago, in my early hiking days. I read reviews, and blogs, and pretty much everyone said it wasn't that great. So, of course I went to try it, and I must say I was pleasantly surprised. I actually quite liked it. Rugged cliffs, medieval ruins, beaches, a Sight of Special Scientific Interest, and all the beach huts. Some of them quite fun. I particularly enjoy the marmite beach hut (I think this is a newer edition, I don't remember it from my first time). I also loved how I could completely switch off and just walk. A good long walk without having to navigate, no risk of getting lost, just following the path along the coast. Another great thing about this walk is you don't have to walk the whole way, you can break it up into bite sized chunks as there are a couple of train stations along the route.

But wait, don't let that put you off.

WHAT TO EXPECT

A lot of promenade and esplanade. Basically, it's a lot of hard ground. But wait, don't let that put you off. The walk starts off along promenade as you make your way through Herne Bay, then after a couple of miles you'll reach the cliffs. Good old rugged cliffs. From there you head up top to reach the Reculver Country Park and Reculver Towers. This is pretty much the only grass of the walk, as after this it's hard path and promenade or esplanade the rest of the way along the coast, with some beaches thrown in. The landscape is also quite flat after the towers, until the 7.5ish mile mark, where you'll be presented with the most unique curvy cliffs I've ever seen. Now, if you want some beach time, most of the way is shingle beach, but there are a few little bays with sand. These sections can be very busy during summer months, however, I find it to be very peaceful and uncrowded on all the bits in between. When you reach Margate, it will likely be quite busy too, but also quite trendy, with lots of places to eat. One thing I particularly like, is the train station is right on the coast. Unlike a lot of other coastal towns in the south east where you need to walk about 10–20 minutes to get to it.

FUN FACT:
The clock tower in Herne Bay is apparently one of the oldest free standing purpose build clock towers in the world.

DIRECTORY

LOGISTICS:

Start/Finish: Herne Bay Station, Margate Station Kent
Difficulty: Easy.
Type: Point to point.
Route Distance: 12.5 miles/20km.
Time: 4h.

HOW TO GET THERE:

Buy a return ticket from London St Pancras or London Victoria to Margate, then get off a few stops earlier at Herne Bay to start the walk. Journey time is similar for both routes, around 1h40min, but the London Victoria route is cheaper. Note: If travelling from St Pancras, make sure you book the correct train. It's the one which goes through Herne Bay first.

COMING BY CAR:

I would modify the walk if coming by car. Park at the Reculver Towers Car park CT6 6SU, then follow the coast east. This would make it an out and back walk. How far you go is up to you. I recommend walking to Minnus Bay and back.

ELEVATION GAIN:

173m/568ft.

TERRAIN:

Lots of concrete, tarmac, grass, maybe shingle.

DOG FRIENDLY:

In parts. Can't go onto the beaches during summer months (1st May–30th Sept), some are all day restrictions, some are between 10am and 6pm. They are allowed on the promenades though.

PHONE SIGNAL:

Yes.

PUBLIC TOILETS:

Yes. At the Reculver Towers, then at each of the beach bay coves along the route. Also at Margate station, or Herne Bay station only during ticket office open hours.

IDEAL TIME OF YEAR:

Anytime is great. Summer if you want to have a dip in the sea and to see the sunflowers. Winter if you like moody vibes and solitude.

OPTION TO SHORTEN THE WALK:

Yes. There are a couple train stations along the route. Birchington-on-Sea and Westgate-on-Sea. Your return ticket will work from these stations. Note: if you are traveling here from St Pancras, that train doesn't stop at Westgate-on-Sea.

WHERE TO EAT?

You'll be walking through a few towns, so there are plenty of options. Here are a few recommendations.

CAFE AND COFFEE:

Herne Bay

- Garage Coffee Roasters (dog friendly).

On the Walk

- 4 miles: HatHats Coffee, Reculver (dog friendly).

Margate

- The Bus Cafe (dogs allowed outside).

RESTAURANT:

On the walk

- 7.5 miles: Minnis Bay Bar and Brasserie (dog friendly).
- 10.5 miles: Finbar's of West Bay (dogs allowed outside).
- 11.5 miles: The St Mildred's Bay (dog friendly).

PUB:

On the walk

- 4 miles: The King Ethelbert Inn (dog friendly).

FOR SUPPLIES:

Tesco, Aldi, Morrisons in Herne Bay and Margate.

TIPS/OTHER THINGS TO KNOW

- I'd wear comfy shoes for this one, trainers for example. There's a lot of hard ground.
- Bring swimwear and towel if you fancy a dip in the sea.
- The beach bays are mostly underwater at high tide, so do the walk when the tide is lower if you want some sandy beach time.
- During summer you might get to see a field full of sunflowers.
- This route is also a cycle path. So you will be joined by cyclists. Or you could even partake if you bring a bike.

make sure the sea stays to your left, and you'll be good.

ROUTE DESCRIPTION

Out of the station turn right. It's now about 10min walk to get to the coast, which you can do following this road. But that's a bit boring, so a short way along you can instead turn to walk through the memorial park on the right, and just follow the signs for the town centre. When you reach the coast, turn right. You'll find the clock tower along here. I've read it chimes on the hour, although, as it so happens I've never been here on the hour so I've not heard it.

Keep going and you'll reach the promenade which you now follow for a good old stretch, with a view to the Reculver Towers ahead. During peak season, this first bit through Herne Bay can be a bit busy, but I find as you get further along the promenade, the crowds die down.

Further along, you'll also notice the green area to your right. If you've had enough of hard ground, you can also walk up through there. There's a few trails, so just make sure the sea stays to your left, and you'll be good.

Staying down on the promenade, you'll then reach the cliffs and warning signs. Basically you don't want to continue this way when the tide is in and sea is rough, also the cliffs are a bit unstable. Just before this point, there is a path which will lead you up to the clifftop, and then along to the Reculver Towers. If you want to stay down here though, you will then have two options…

Walk to the Reculver Towers

Keep going for a bit to reach the wooden bridge. If the tide is out you can stay down here to reach the Reculver towers. First on a dirt trail with the cliffs looming above to the right, then on shingle, or if the tide is out far enough, sand. Best only do this if the tide is way out or on its way out. This whole area is underwater at high tide, and you don't want to walk right below the cliffs due to their crumbly nature.

The other option, which is very lovely, is to walk on clifftop. So just over the bridge, head up the steps and keep going all the way up to reach a green, where you turn left. Continue through a bush tree tunnel, and you will reach a big open meadow type field. Up here there are two trails you can take. The left is the coast path trail, and to the right is the Oyster Bay Trail. I recommend the right. It's a very nice wide grass trail with a lovely view to the Reculver Towers, as you make your way towards them.

The Reculver Towers

These are ruins of 12th century church towers, and a Roman Fort dating back to the third century. It's one of the earliest forts built to protect against invasion from the Saxons. This is also the 4 mile mark, and a good place to stop for a snack break. You can pick up something from HatHats Coffee, then go sit on the green by the towers.

Walk to Minnis Bay

Continue past the towers, then left to get onto the northern sea wall path along the coast. It's now a good long stretch of this. A straight line of hard path as far as the eye can see. I find there is a sort of charm, in the uniformity of it. It's along this stretch where during the summer you might get to see the massive sunflower field.

After what feels like an eternity, the scenery changes a little, as the path curves you around a bit through the marshy wetland.

Eventually you'll reach the promenade around Minnis Bay (note, you have to walk down the steps to it). The beach is shingle at first, but then becomes sandy further along, with all the cafes and stuff. You can also stay on the path you were on, which will give you a lovely view overlooking the beach huts.

This is the 7.5 mile mark. From here you can get the train from Birchinton-on-Sea.

Walk to Westgate-on-Sea

Past Minnis Bay you'll see the curvy white cliffs ahead, along the Birchington promenade. Basically head that way. If it was busy in Minnis Bay, it won't be around here. I've walked along here during the height of summer on a weekend, and the difference in the amount of people is quite remarkable. Almost suffocatingly busy around Minnis Bay, then literally a handful on this path around the cliffs.

Pretty unique cliffs by the way. Short and curvy, alongside the wide promenade. Further along, the curviness of the cliffs intensifies with houses lining the clifftop. It must be quite expensive to live up there.

After about 1.5 miles, the promenade ends and you need to walk up to the clifftop. Unfortunately it's not so nice now as you'll be following the road for a bit. Longer than is desirable I'm afraid, well, about half a mile, to reach Westgate Bay. Where you'll be back on promenade or esplanade, one of them, with another stretch of sandy beach, beach huts, and maybe crowds of people.

Now if you keep going, around the next headland, you'll reach St Mildred's Bay. Another sandy beach section, with all the beach huts. Including the marmite beach hut.

This is the 10.5–11.5 mile mark. You can stop (or start) the walk at either of these bays, via Westgate-on-Sea station.

Walk to Margate

You'll then be on the Westbrook Promenade which will lead you all the way to Margate. So you know how I said the sections of the walk between the beaches are very uncrowded. That doesn't apply here. You're in Margate now, which is a hugely popular summer destination. You'll first pass Westbrook Bay, with another good old sandy beach, before reaching Margate Main Sands, which is where you'll find the train station.

Follow Zoe Tehrani as the adventure continues:

along the dramatic shores of the South West Coast Path, through Yorkshire's rolling moors and timeless villages, across the tranquil lakes of Cumbria, past the golden coves of Cornwall and the rugged charm of Devon, into the wild heart of Wales, and onward to the majestic highlands and breathtaking vistas of Scotland... and beyond.